THE FOODS OF CHICAGO

A Delicious History

G. Bradley Publishing, Inc., St. Louis, Missouri • www.gbradleypublishing.com

This publication is a companion project to WTTW11 Chicago's public television station's documentary *The Foods of Chicago: A Delicious History*. The program was written and produced by Dan Protess and hosted by Geoffrey Baer.

PUBLICATION STAFF

Writers:
Historical Essays . . . . Diane Gannon
Personal Profiles: . . . . .Gloria Baraks
. . . . Mark Weinstein
. . . . Liz Roy
Food Photography . . . . Katherine Bish
Recipe Editor . . . . Catherine Lambrecht
Chicago Foodways Roundtable
Photo Editor. . . . . .Michael Bruner
Book Design. . . . . .Diane Kramer
Dust Jacket Design . . . . .Michael Bruner
Project Coordinator . . . . Diane Gannon
Copy Editors: . . . . Gloria Baraks
. . . . Blake Baraks
Publisher. . . . . . . .G. Bradley Publishing, Inc.

DEDICATION

It is with overwhelming pride that we dedicate this book to all Chicago immigrants. Their indomitable spirit led them to embark on a new life. Leaving their home, friends and family, they overcame all odds against them. They not only bettered their own lives, they have enriched the City of Chicago.

A graduate of Eastern Illinois University School of Journalism, Katherine Bish has been telling stories through pictures since 1998. Her award-winning food photography is regularly featured in *St. Louis Magazine* and the *St. Louis Post-Dispatch*. Her work has also been featured in *National Geographic Traveler, Food and Wine, Gourmet* and *Bon Appetit*. Katherine was the food photographer for the *Greektown Chicago, German Milwaukee* and *Polish Chicago* books by G. Bradley Publishing.

Go to <u>www.gbradleypublishing.com</u> for other books of interest

Italian St. Louis
by Eleanore Berra Marfisi

Greek Chicago
by Alexa Ganakos

German Milwaukee
by Trudy Paradis

Polish Chicago
by Joseph Zurawski

ISBN 978-0-9774512-5-8
Printed in the U.S.A.

TABLE OF CONTENTS

THE MAKING OF
The Foods of Chicago: A Delicious History

This book is a companion to the television program of the same name produced by WTTW11, Chicago's public television station. Producer/writer Dan Protess and I spent the summer of 2007 eating our way through Chicago history as we explored the contributions of different ethnic groups and the origins of traditional Chicago favorites. Dozens of restaurants and private individuals welcomed us into their kitchens. We also visited enormous food factories and recorded the making of everything from the famous Vienna Beef hot dog to Tootsie Rolls (they make 60 million of them per day). Dan summed up our goal this way: "I wanted this show to be a celebration of Chicago's cultural diversity, because I think that's what makes this such a terrific place to live. And I really couldn't think of a better window into Chicago's diverse communities than food."   --Geoffrey Baer, WTTW Chicago

For more information about the program including how to obtain a DVD visit www.wttw.com/foodsofchicago.

In 1896, Austrian immigrant to Chicago Leo Hirshfield names his chocolate creation after his five-year-old daughter, whose nick name was "Tootsie."

Cameraman Tim Boyd uses his head to get a good camera angle for the making of Polish sausage at Bobak Sausage Company.

Dan and Geoffrey discuss production plans with Chris Pacelli.

Ray Kroc from Oak Park turned a simple idea into a mega franchise food operation. His first location was in Des Plaines in 1955.

Host Geoffrey Baer (left) and Producer/Writer Dan Protess (center) with Richard Gordon at Chocolate Potpourri. Big smiles and silly hairnets are required for sampling gourmet chocolate truffles fresh off the factory line.

Host Geoffrey Baer and cameraman, Tim Boyd, interview Art Velasquez, president of Azteca Foods, in the factory where tortillas are made.

Chris Pacelli, owner of Al's Italian Beef, (right) gives host Geoffrey Baer a lesson in the proper technique for eating the iconic sandwich that his family has been serving since 1938.

In 1943, Ike Sewell started a tradition when he introduced the Chicago Deep Dish Pizza at Pizza Uno at 29 East Ohio.

Twinkies were invented in 1930 by James Dewar at his Continental Baking store in Schiller Park.

Editor Paul Thornton (right) works with writer/producer Dan Protess to put the show together in the editing room. In total the editing process took close to three months.

In 1941, Greek immigrant, Leo Stefanos, named his new candy store after a symbol of peace— a dove holding an olive branch.

White Sox players enjoy Chicago-style hot dogs at Comisky Park in 1930.

Producer/writer Dan Protess (center) with cameraman Tim Boyd videotaping African American items from the collection of Donna Pierce (seated) food writer for the Chicago Tribune.

Flaming Saganaki elicits a round of "Opaa" from patrons at the Parthenon and other restaurants in Greektown.

A talented member of Chicago's West Indian Folk Dance Company.

Dimitri William Moore

"It was the best of times, it was the worst of times." Charles Dickens' opening line in his epic novel, *A Tale of Two Cities*, might have proven to be just as fitting an introduction had his subject matter been the African American experience in Chicago, rather than the French Revolution. Indeed, the Chicago African American story is one highlighted by brilliant artistic and political achievement, but marred by a continuous history of wrongful discrimination.

African Americans played a role in Chicago history even before there was a Chicago, as they accompanied French fur traders to the shores of Lake Michigan as far back as the 1780s. The arrival of the American Republic and its southern slave states brought many more African Americans to Chicago during the first 60 years of the 19th century, as many slaves escaping southern plantations and freedmen alike found their way north to Chicago. Immediately prior to the Civil War, approximately 1,000 African Americans called Chicago home. However, though Chicago was a center of the abolitionist movement, before and during the Civil War, African American Chicagoans did not possess full civil rights as they could not vote in elections or testify against whites in Chicago.

In the aftermath of the Civil War and with the passage of the 13th, 14th and 15th Amendments to the United States Constitution, enslaved African Americans were given their freedom and all were granted civil and voting rights. During the Reconstruction years, some African Americans utilized some of these rights, but as the Union Army ended their occupation of the South, so did these newfound rights disappear for southern

African Americans. As a strongly segregated South began to take shape, many more African Americans migrated north to Chicago in the 1870s and '80s.

During those same years institutional segregation began to disappear in Chicago and the State of Illinois enacted laws that gave African Americans the right to vote in state elections, forbade school segregation and prohibited public displays of discrimination. The situation in Chicago was certainly an improvement to that of the South, but African American Chicagoans faced great struggles nonetheless as there existed no laws to combat employment or housing discrimination. Therefore, though Chicago's African American community contained strong and increasing middle and upper class segments populated by businessmen and professionals, many were relegated to the ranks of domestic servants and manual labor. Furthermore, Chicago area landlords habitually discriminated against would-be African American tenants, either refusing them outright or charging them extra rent. Thus, by 1910, 78% of the African Americans in Chicago lived on the South Side of the city in an area known as The Black Belt, which ran for more than 30 blocks along State Street and was full of substandard, overcrowded housing.

However, even under these decidedly imperfect circumstances, southern African Americans still continued to migrate north from the overt racial hostilities that persisted in the South well into the second half of the 20th century, thereby bringing the African American population of Chicago to 40,000 by 1910. Moreover, despite the struggles every African American Chicagoan had to face, the late 19th and early 20th century proved to be a time of great political activism for the community.

For example, in 1878 African American attorney Ferdinand L. Barnett founded *The Conservator*, Chicago's first newspaper for his community which advocated aggressively combating racial inequality. Ida B. Wells, who was to become Attorney Barnett's wife in 1895, fought to end the vile practice of lynching. From her home base in Chicago, she also advocated women's voting rights and played a significant role in founding the National Association for the Advancement of Colored People (NAACP). African American Chicagoans also started local offices of the NAACP and the Urban League, created several newspapers, including the *Chicago Defender*, and founded Provident Hospital. Further, several politicians ran successful city campaigns, thereby making Chicago home to the strongest African American political organization in the United States at the time.

World War I brought economic opportunities to the African American community of Chicago and beyond, as military conscription and war-inspired immigration restrictions took away current white male workers and cut off access to European immigrant labor. Thus, out of necessity, industry hired African American workers for the first time. The *Chicago Defender* spread the word of the labor shortage, and between 1916 and 1920, over 50,000 African Americans migrated to Chicago to take advantage of industry need.

The southern immigrants not only received bigger paychecks than most had ever received in their lives in the rural South of the early 20th century, they also found a community alive with

Chicago History Museum

Children on the stoop at 162 West Erie Street. Between 1916 and 1920, over 50,000 African Americans migrated to Chicago in response to industry need.

A quilting class was a popular event in the 1930s. Good conversations were part of the fun.

The Plantation Café was located on 35 State Street, five blocks east of "The Stroll," where some of Chicago's great jazz bands played in the 1920s.

A statue of Harold Washington, Chicago's first African American mayor.

A beautiful mural in Bronzeville, celebrating some of Chicago's best African American musicians.

musical and artistic inspiration. It was during these years that Chicago jazz started to come into its own. Moreover, during the 1910s and '20s, African Americans found excellent jobs in city government offices, while more were elected to city office than ever before. Despite being in the midst of progress, deep-seated racism showed its face as was always the case of the African American experience in Chicago. For instance, with the general exception of the meatpacking and garment industries, African Americans were kept out of most industrial trade unions. Because of housing shortages and discrimination, the majority still lived in The Black Belt and, to make matters worse, their attempts to move into white neighborhoods were usually met with swift and often violent responses, including a riot in 1919 which left 23 African American Chicagoans dead and 300 injured.

The arrival of the Great Depression exacerbated the racist tendencies in general Chicago society and, as was the case with other marginalized groups of the era, African American employees tended to be among the first to receive a pink slip. The employment discrimination reached such a level that by 1939 half of these families were receiving government assistance.

Yet, remarkably, the oppression of the Depression years inspired a tremendous literary and artistic revival, later titled the Chicago Black Renaissance. From this deep well of talent and inspiration sprang striking paintings, profound novels and groundbreaking poetry that focused upon the realities of African American urban life.

World War II brought new labor shortages

and renewed African American immigration. From 1940 to 1960, hundreds of thousands of African Americans migrated north to Chicago, bringing their population from 278,000 to 813,000 in just 20 years. As was the case for World War I migrants, the new immigrants found a bustling Chicago with well-paying industrial jobs, a vibrant rhythm and blues scene and strong African American politicians.

However, they still faced employment discrimination in retail, fire and police departments, as well as construction. They also were still confronted with housing discrimination and shortages, a situation made worse by the influx into already stressed African American neighborhoods.

The housing problems were significant enough to attract the attention of major civil rights leaders such as Dr. Martin Luther King, Jr. Unfortunately, even Dr. King could not fully solve the shortage which still exists today, despite continued efforts by the city of Chicago and local African American activists to correct it.

Yet, there is another side to this coin, as shown by the political rise of Harold Washington, Chicago's first African American mayor in the 1980s. Also prominent are the DuSable Museum of African American History and Chicago's incredibly vital artistic, musical and cultural scene.

While the struggle to completely eradicate racial discrimination is not yet over, by their amazing strength, creativity and ability to endure, the African Americans of Chicago have shown that they are up to any challenge.

Chicago Blues musician, Carl Weathersby, at the 2007 Chicago Blues Festival.

Sean Birmingham

Above: An African American family living at 849 North Wells Street in 1949. Long-term housing shortages in Chicago forced many African Americans to endure challenging living conditions. Right: Three generations pose for a photograph outside of their home in 1931. The Chicago Black Renaissance took flight during the difficult years of the Depression, inspiring an artistic and literary revival in Chicago's African American community.

Chicago History Museum

Jesse White Tumbling Team

A thrilling performance of the Jesse White Tumbling Team. Shown at the far right of the photo, Jesse White is Illinois's first African American Secretary of State. Secretary White founded his internationally known tumbling team in 1959, and for the past 47 years has not only trained team members in the tumbling arts, but has helped them reach personal success.

ROBERT ADAMS, JR. & SR.

My mother's father was nicknamed "Honey." It suited him just fine and suited the name of our restaurant Honey1 BBQ, originally founded in Austin on the west side of Chicago. My father, Robert Adams Sr., and our family opened Honey1 four years ago and it's been going ever since. My dad is a great cook and he's been at it for over 30 years, not only for his family at home but also for company parties.

My mother, Patricia, is the author of our fabulous sauce. She made it with the idea of "not too sweet or not too hot! Just right." That's why we've been in business so long because we put our family's soul into the cooking.

I can't begin to tell you what a wonderful feeling it is to have a customer come up after dinner and tell us how much they love our food. Being the only "real" wood smokers, now on the north side, we are very lucky to have the Bucktown neighborhood behind us.

I am African American, born and raised in Mariana, Arkansas. My grandparents taught me the fine art of making meat and when I came to Chicago I brought the knowledge with me to share with the great folks in this city.

The secret to our recipe is – very little. We put absolutely nothing on our meat except maybe a bit of meat seasoning and that's about it. You can have the sauce on the meat or on the side. We smoke it very slowly over wood only, and that's what makes our place so different. Taking time, taking pride – that's what we're all about.

BBQ Spare Ribs

INGREDIENTS:

"Full slab" spareribs (or roughly 2½ lbs.)

Spice Supreme Seasoned Meat Tenderizer (available at Moo & Oink)

Honey 1 BBQ Sauce (available at Honey 1)

White or red oak

DIRECTIONS:

Wash, trim and cut off tips of ribs, then sprinkle with a little Spice Supreme Seasoned Meat Tenderizer. Place ribs directly on rack and slow smoke using red or white oak. Slow-cook slab of spareribs for three hours in order to reach smoky perfection.

Plate the spareribs. Cole slaw, french fries or potato salad make a great side dish.

ROBERT SENIOR'S SLOW-COOKING TIPS

To slow-smoke pork tips, chicken, or hot links, they must spend a required 2½ hours on the rack. A pork butt requires 10-13 hours such that, when you pull it apart slowly, it is good and tender (if you see that the meat has been cut apart, not shredded, then it's a dead giveaway that it's only been cooked for 5-6 hours).

A little cherrywood is a nice addition. Hickory wood makes meat taste bitter. The sweetest taste and smell is derived from the wood of an apple tree.

WILBERT JONES

My grandmother worked as a cook for an Italian family in Clarksdale, Mississippi for over 40 years. I remember many of the wonderful dishes she prepared, and corn pudding, a baked custard side dish, was one of my favorites. She added cheeses like mozzarella and parmesan, the latter being a very versatile ingredient substitute common to the South in those days. It is a dish similar to Native American "corn pone" (an eggless corn bread batter baked in small pans, fried in a skillet or baked over hot ashes). Whenever I want some excellent soul food and don't want to cook it myself I wander over to Edna Stewart's restaurant on the west side of Chicago. Edna makes smothered chicken, collard greens, macaroni and cheese, and coconut cake, just the way I like it; all from scratch. It feels like visiting my grandmother all over again.

Many people think I have come a long way from my roots. I am the president of Healthy Concepts, a food and beverage product development and marketing company. I have authored three published cookbooks and my New Soul Food Cookbook *won the Purple Reflection Award from the National Council of Negro Women. I have contributed my expertise and recipes to books by Art Smith (Oprah Winfrey's personal chef) and written articles for* Prepared Food Magazine *and BET.com. One of my finest moments, however, was being the first African American to be inducted into the prestigious Les Amis d'Escoffier Society of Chicago. Yet, it is my roots which have helped to shape who I am today and Chicago was a perfect place for them to take wing.*

What can I say – Chicago is my kind of town as it is rich in culture, people and cuisine. I love the seasons, (some folks say we have only two seasons, winter and summer,) and I partake in the numerous festivals and city-sponsored events. Chicago has the best architecture, a great lakefront and nothing beats the magnificent views from the John Hancock Building.

12

Wilbert's great-great-grandmother Julia Mae Hogan.

CORN PUDDING

INGREDIENTS

2 cups fresh corn kernels (about 3-4 ears)

1 tbsp. all-purpose flour

2 tbsp. sugar

½ tsp. salt

¼ tsp. black pepper

2 eggs, lightly beaten

1 cup milk

2 tbsp. butter, melted

2 tbsp. bread crumbs

¼ tsp. sweet paprika

Preheat oven to 325F. Place ½ cup of corn kernels in a blender and whirl until puréed. Pour mixture in a large bowl along with remaining corn kernels, flour, sugar, salt and pepper. Stir in eggs, milk and melted butter. Pour mixture into a 9-inch buttered baking pan. Sprinkle bread crumbs and paprika over the top of the mixture. Place the 9-inch pan into an 11-inch baking pan (filled with two cups of water). Then, carefully set the 11-inch baking pan (with the 9-inch baking pan) in the oven and bake 40-45 minutes or until pudding is set (a knife inserted in the center comes out clean).

SERVES 4-6

KOCOA WINBUSH

We all know that the sweet potato is indigenous to America. However, close relatives of this potato were brought over to the New World by those of African ancestry. As a younger person, I was not fond of sweet potato pie because it tasted heavy as lead, so I avoided my grandmother (photo opposite page) Gussie Benning's recipe. After I attended chef's school, "Gaga" (grandmother) shared her egg custard recipe, at right, with me. She explained that my great-great-grandmother had worked as an adult slave in the "big house." She cooked for the slave master's taste buds, not hers. The addition of egg custard happened when more expensive food products found in plantation houses were added as compared to the "heavy as lead" versions of this pie eaten by slaves.

Etched on my hard-as-stone head is Gaga's reflection that black folk have an understanding of food which transcends the "soul" label erroneously attached to us. The abilities of African American cooks are not limited to food which is "soul inspired." Our "mammies," as chefs in plantation houses, became masters of international (English, French, Italian, German, Greek) cuisine. This talent was passed on to future generations as they continued to recreate dishes from any number of diverse backgrounds.

Okay, okay, I can feel my ears burning! I hear y'all saying, "I can't eat that rich pie. All those eggs and butter in there; my heart can't take it." So, to show that I can "switch hit," here's the low-fat, low-cholesterol version.

Sweet Potato Pie "Lite" — Decrease butter to a half stick and omit egg custard. Lighten potato purée with whipped egg whites (four for this recipe). Lessen sugar to one-half cup or use sugar substitute. Use pre-made crusts (refrigerated or frozen). Proceed with same baking instructions.

THE SWEET POTATO PIE EXPERIENCE

INGREDIENTS

FILLING

4 lbs. sweet potatoes
4 tbsp. fresh lemon juice
1 stick butter
1 cup sugar
2 tsp. vanilla extract
¼ tsp. allspice
½ tsp. cinnamon
⅛ tsp. fresh nutmeg, grated

PIE CRUST

1¼ cups whole wheat pastry flour
1¼ cups all-purpose flour
1 tsp. nutmeg
1 tsp. ground cinnamon
½ tsp. salt
5 tbsp. vegetable shortening (solid and cold)
5 tbsp. butter (cold), cut into small pieces
6-8 tbsp. ice water
2 pie tins

CUSTARD

4 eggs
½-¾ cup milk or cream
1 tbsp. sugar
Pinch nutmeg, freshly ground

SWEET POTATO FILLING: Boil sweet potatoes with skins on (there are two pounds of potatoes per pie). Peel and mash while still warm. Season with fresh lemon juice (to retain bright color) and add butter, vanilla extract, allspice, cinnamon and nutmeg. Taste to adjust seasonings if necessary. Although you want the filling sweet, you also want to experience a slight tart bite from the lemon juice.

PIE CRUST: In a large bowl, combine flours, nutmeg, cinnamon and salt; blend well. Cut in shortening with a pastry blender until it resembles a coarse meal. Cut in butter until mixture resembles small peas.

Sprinkle most of ice water over flour, then gently mix with a fork to bring dough together. Work dough as little as possible. Form into a ball, divide in half and wrap each piece with plastic wrap. Refrigerate at least one hour before rolling out to use.

CUSTARD: Make a custard of eggs and milk (or cream). Whisk until incorporated then add sugar and nutmeg. Take ⅓ of sweet potato filling and mix (temper) with ⅓ of custard. It is important to taste as you add the custard so that the custard does not dilute the flavor of the filling. You add custard to lighten the mixture, not alter the taste. Once you find your hit, fill unbaked pie crusts and bake at 375F for 45-60 minutes, depending on how deep your pie tins are.

SERVES 12-16

15

Richie Diesterheft

CHINESE

Today the Chicagoland area is home to a tremendously hardworking, entrepreneurially savvy and culturally vibrant Chinese American community. They are professionals, business owners and university students, and their contributions have immeasurably enriched the Windy City. However, the Chinese journey to this point has, sadly, been long and littered with obstacles of discrimination of which most European immigrants never had to face.

The first Chinese immigrants to cross the Pacific for American shores arrived in California in the 1850s. This almost exclusively male group generally hailed from the Guangdong Province of southern China, the inhabitants of which have historically been called Cantonese. During the mid-19th century this region experienced a horrendous combination of disasters, including economic depression, floods, famines, peasant uprisings and interethnic wars. Such terrible conditions provided sufficient cause for many able-bodied Cantonese to look outside of their ancestral region for something better. Some heard of gold strikes and booming economies in the American West and set sail for California.

Most of these immigrants hoped to earn good money in a land hungry for workers and return to China wealthier men. As such, they were willing to work in some of the most difficult and dangerous jobs the American West had to offer, including agriculture, mining, and in particular, the railroad. Indeed, the western half of the Transcontinental Railroad was built in very large part on the backs of Chinese laborers.

Initially, the settlements of the American West welcomed these Chinese workers, as the rate of growth for the booming Western economy had outpaced the growth of the available labor market. But when the unregulated, "boom or bust" economy of the American West faltered, the minority Chinese became easy scapegoats.

As a result, the Chinese suffered from all manner of discrimination, ranging from racist violence to codified discrimination in both state and federal laws. Indeed, not only did the State of California, the port of entry for many

Chinese, pass anti-Chinese laws during the 19th century, the national Democratic and Republican parties both included exclusion planks in their party platforms in the election of 1880, in an effort to please vocal labor leaders who desired a block on further Chinese immigration. These forces achieved their discriminatory goal when President Chester Arthur signed the first Chinese Exclusion Act in 1882, thereby making the Chinese the first ethnic group in the United States to be excluded from entry or naturalization on the basis of race or ethnicity.

Even worse, during the 19th century the Chinese had to endure many instances of racist mob violence. Some of the particularly terrible incidents include the lynching of 17 Chinese in Los Angeles in 1871, the murder of 28 Chinese in race riots at Rock Springs, Wyoming in 1885, and the attempted deportation of Seattle's Chinese population in 1886.

Nevertheless, Chinese immigrants found ways to survive and even thrive. While the vast majority of Chinese decided to stay in the west, the tightening economy in those parts coupled with ongoing racial hostility caused more than one enterprising group of Chinese to travel east along the rails their people had laid down, and those rails, like the proverbial Roman roads, eventually all led to Chicago. A predominantly immigrant city, the Chinese, with their small numbers, were a relatively inconspicuous addition.

By 1880, 172 Chinese lived in Chicago. Over the next 40 years, a period when millions of Europeans poured into Chicago, the Chinese, enduring the burden of the exclusion laws, saw their population grow at a glacial pace. By 1920, only 2,353 Chinese called Chicago home.

As a result, the growth of Chicago's Chinese community was stunted and thrown out of balance. In the face of such institutional hostility, many immigrants returned to China. Moreover, because most of the original immigrants were men, and since the exclusion laws not only generally prohibited non-citizen Chinese men from sending for family or wives, but actually presumed a Chinese woman traveling alone was a prostitute, it became impossible for the Chinese to do what almost every immigrant group would do, namely, to build a family-centered ethnic community. In fact, even as late as 1926, only 6% of the total Chicago Chinese community was comprised of women. This demographic imbalance just enhanced the European-descended majority's sense of "otherness" with regard to the Chinese community, thereby further fanning the flames of racial hostility.

Racist restrictive covenants often kept them from owning property, while discriminatory employment practices prevented a majority of Chinese from being hired by local industry. In order to keep themselves financially afloat, many Chinese opened laundries. Though requiring little initial

A Chinese immigrant family in 1904.

Chinatown's Clark Street, looking north from Harrison Street, in 1908.

Facing page: Chicago's Chinatown, present day.

investment or specialized knowledge, the Chinese found a niche in laundries, as they were deemed unattractive businesses by the general public due to the enormous amount of manual labor involved prior to mechanization. Other Chinese made their way by opening restaurants. Further, many decided to live in non-Chinese neighborhoods over their laundries or restaurants, so as to not present a target for mass hatred as a Chinatown might.

Nevertheless, despite the potential for antagonism, a number of Chinese did choose to work and sometimes live in Chinese-dominant neighborhoods. The first Chinatown grew up in the 1880s near the intersection of Clark and Van Buren and became a Chinese commercial center with cigar makers, Asian goods' suppliers, groceries, and restaurants. By the 1910s, a conflict between rival factions in the community led to a split, and by 1913, the majority of the Chinese community relocated to the present-day location of Cermak Road and Wentworth.

Chinese immigrants also created several organizations to improve the lives of their fellow countrymen. The Chicago branch of the powerful Chinese Consolidated Benevolent Association, founded in 1906, settled disputes, provided social services, certified official documents and served as the guardian of law and order. In the same vein, family associations provided much needed support and protection to members, while also keeping native cultural traditions alive.

In 1943, Congress repealed the Chinese Exclusion Act as a gesture of solidarity with America's ally in the Pacific Theater during World War II. However, because fears of mass Asian immigration played a dominant role in the debate, only 50 Chinese were permitted to enter the U.S. each year. Nevertheless, the repeal opened the door at long last to naturalization and the vote. Along with naturalization came the ability for families long separated by the policy curtain to reunite at last.

In 1949, when Mao Zedong transformed a post-WWII China still recovering from the horrors of Japanese occupation into the People's Republic of China, thousands more fled the Communist state and were accepted into the United States as displaced persons under more lenient federal refugee standards in the post-war era. However, the immigrants who arrived from China in the 1950s included both men and women who tended to be Mandarin-speaking, educated professionals,

Jeremy Atherton

Beautiful ladies celebrating Chinese New Year in Chicago's Chinatown in 2007.

Top right: Golden Nine Dragon Wall; A Shortened Version of Beijing's Forbidden City's Glazed Tile Wall in Chicago's Chinatown.

Bottom right: Willie Moy's Hand Laundry, at 4953 South Ashland Avenue, a longtime Chicago business.

Richie Diesterheft

Chicago History Museum

whereas the immigrants of the 19th century were, for the most part, Cantonese-speaking men who had received little formal education.

The influx caused Chinatown's population to boom; overcrowding quickly became an issue. When restrictive covenants and barriers to employment began to fall in the civil rights' era, Chinese flocked to the suburbs seeking better opportunities for education, housing and employment.

In the 1950s and '60s, when America needed technical talent to fill its need for engineers and technicians in a growing technological economy, it found them in the highly educated professional classes from Hong Kong and Taiwan resulting in what was called the "brain drain." After the enactment of the Immigration and Nationality Act of 1965, which allowed for dramatically increased quotas for Chinese immigrants, and after President Nixon's visit to China in 1973, more mainland Chinese started arriving in Chicago. Moreover, after the conclusion of the wars in Southeast Asia in the mid 1970s, many ethnic Chinese from those regions immigrated as well.

This latter group established a Chinatown in Uptown, creating a vibrant, international community. In addition, renewed waves of investment and development have revived the Chinatown at Wentworth and Cermak Road.

As many Chinese still arrive in Chicago with every passing year, the conclusion of the Chinese immigration story is still yet to be told, but if the past is prologue, it should be a story of tremendous efforts, strength, tenacity and success in the face of incredible obstacles.

Jeremy Atherton

A delightful young dragon at 2004's Chinese New Year's celebration.

Chicago History Museum

Chicago History Museum

Chinese City Hall on Wentworth Avenue.

Chicago History Museum

Chinese citizens registering for the draft in Chicago.

A parade in Chinatown in 1928.

WEN HUANG
MONICA ENG

CHILI PASTE MANTO SANDWICH

INGREDIENTS

2 lbs. fresh red or green
   jalapeno peppers
½ lb. ground beef
1 lb. whole peanuts
1 lb. whole walnuts

3 oz. sesame seeds
3 tsp. rice wine (or Chinese
   cooking wine)
2 tsp. sugar
1 tsp. MSG

6 tsp. plum sauce
1 oz. ginger
3-4 tsp. salt
16 oz. vegetable oil

Grind peanuts and walnuts in a food processor. Wash whole peppers and ginger. Wipe them dry and chop them in food processor. Heat four ounces of vegetable oil in a frying pan then cook ground beef until well-done. Put aside.

Heat four ounces vegetable oil, add nuts and sesame seeds, then keep stirring for three minutes and place to one side. Heat remaining oil; add ginger and plum sauce, then the peppers. Cook for about three minutes on a medium flame, stirring constantly.

Mix ground beef and nuts into peppers. Add sugar, MSG and wine, then keep stir-frying for another four minutes. Adjust salt, sugar, MSG and plum sauce to taste. Cool and distribute into jars. Store in refrigerator.

SERVES 20

My late father considered rice a southern idiosyncrasy. We lived in northern China and ate lots of steamed noodles and steamed buns called "manto." If he had rice for dinner, he had to eat a manto afterward complaining that rice was not filling. In the 1970s, the Communist government assigned every family each month a ration of meat, eggs and cooking oil. In the winter, when she could not use vegetables, my mother ground dry chili peppers with hot oil and we would grab a manto from the steamer and make a chili sandwich.

At boarding school I would smuggle in a small jar of chili paste because no homemade food was allowed for fear the students would be spoiled with "bourgeois" habits. My friends and I hid in our dorm and made bourgeois sandwiches out of fresh buns from the cafeteria.

Hardship food is back in vogue in China. My sister, who lives in the city of Xian in northwest China, dug out my mother's recipe and enriched it with peanuts, walnuts, sesame and ground beef, all ingredients unheard of during the difficult years of the 1970s. Her friends loved it. Each year she buys

three pounds of peppers to make 20 to 30 jars of the chili paste for family and friends. Thus, a new tradition has been born.

Though I have lived in the U.S. for 17 years, I still crave the spicy, salty and oily manto sandwich. With the help of Monica Eng, a food writer in Chicago, we tried my sister's recipe. I suffered a terrible sneeze attack while grinding the jalapeno, but the end result was very rewarding. The spicy flavor brings back memories of those tough, teenage years. The sweet, rich and crunchy taste of the added ingredients reminds me how much my life has changed.

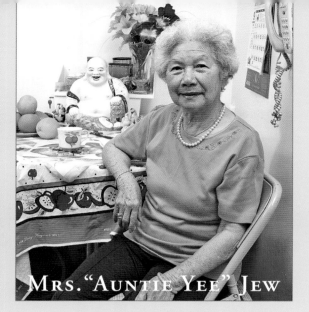

MRS. "AUNTIE YEE" JEW

"Gung fu" does not necessarily refer to the martial art but any skill requiring time and hard work. Coming from the Guangdong Province in southern China to America in the 1950s to join my husband, I have experienced gung fu. Chicago was disorienting because I knew few people, couldn't speak the language and was very homesick. I got lost many times and the snow was so cold. But what made it home was bringing the Toisan recipes here and using my skill to bring alive the pungent tastes of China.

This recipe came down to me from many generations through my mother. I like to prepare dishes like fish and spare ribs using steam, which is a traditional skill. Simple ingredients such as ginger, salted black beans, soy sauce and garlic preserve the freshness and original sweetness of the ingredients.

I am not so young and inexperienced now and I laugh to think how simple I was back when I came to this country. There are a lot more Chinese here now — there is laughter, there is talk, there is vibrance. My old life in Hong Kong seems so far away.

22

HAHM HAH JERNG CHOW FAHN
(SALTED SHRIMP PASTE FRIED RICE)

INGREDIENTS

5 oz. char siu (Chinese barbecued pork loin, available at any Chinese barbecue shop) or diced ham

¼ cup peas and carrots, frozen

2 green onions, chopped finely

2 eggs, scrambled, fried as a thin omelette and sliced into strips

1 tsp. hahm hah jerng (salted shrimp paste)

2 cups cold steamed rice

1 tsp. light soy sauce

Salt and pepper to taste

2 tbsp. vegetable oil (for frying)

· ·

The rice can be prepared in advance and then air-cooled or refrigerated. Rice should not be hot, because the humidity will not produce good fried rice.

Heat oil in a pan or a wok for two minutes. The oil should not be smoking hot, just hot, then lower heat to medium. Into the oil add the cha siu, hahm hah jerng, egg strips, and rice then stir constantly. Salted shrimp paste is a strong flavor which, for some, is an acquired taste. Use a scant amount at first then, if you like, add more. Fried rice is extremely flexible to absorb a lot or a little.

The rice, which is normally sticky, will begin to separate into individual grains; then the rice will begin to pop up a bit from the bottom as they're frying in oil.

Once everything's separate and slightly jumpy, add peas and carrots, which are there for color, until they're warmed through. Finish with green onions, soy sauce, salt and pepper. These are added last for the aroma and color they impart to the dish.

SERVES 4-6

JACKIE SHEN

I have always enjoyed potstickers, a horn-shaped food item that dates back to the Song Dynasty in 1000 A.D. As a child, I was told they resembled a gold nugget, symbolizing household wealth. We often ate potstickers around Chinese festivals or the New Year, as my mother would make a hundred of them. For me, potstickers recall the good times we had as a family.

Worldwide, food is the universal language. To love another person by offering what you have, usually food, is the common denominator. Growing up in Hong Kong, my parents were always hosting weekend parties. I would help prior to each party and watch my mother's preparation.

I came to the United States when I was 17. I studied hotel/restaurant managment at the University of Houston. To pay for tuition, I worked summers in Chicago. I fell in love with this city, so I returned after graduation.

Great jobs have come and gone; currently, I am the executive chef for Red Light. The constant in my life—cooking for the people of Chicago—brings me great joy. This town has given me the opportunity to match its image, that of a city of excellence.

24

GYOZA (POTSTICKERS)

FILLING

2 tbsp. minced water
    chestnuts or jicama
½ lb. ground pork
4 tbsp. scallions (white
    part only), minced
½ tsp. sesame oil
2 tbsp. soy sauce
½ tsp. ginger, minced
½ tsp. garlic, minced
¼ tsp. salt

GYOZA

3 tbsp. vegetable oil,
    divided, or as needed
30 (about 3 ½-inch)
    round gyoza wrappers
    (available in Asian
    and Japanese markets)
Teriyaki sauce
Sweet chile sauce, as needed

GYOZA: Combine filling ingredients. Place one portion of filling in the center of each gyoza. Moisten the edges with water. Fold over in a half-moon shape and pleat the edges three times with your thumbs. Then, taking the dumpling from the pleated top, press down to flatten the bottom. Spray a large baking sheet with vegetable oil spray and, as the dumplings are filled and shaped, place them on the baking sheet.

In a ten-inch nonstick skillet, heat one tablespoon of vegetable oil over medium heat. Add as many gyoza, bottom side down, as the skillet will comfortably hold

without crowding; about ten. Cook over medium heat for two minutes then add two tablespoons of water. Cover and steam until the filling is cooked and the bottom of each gyoza is golden brown; about four minutes. Remove cover and turn all the gyoza on one side and cook to lightly brown; 1-2 minutes. Repeat on the other side; 1-2 minutes. Serve immediately or keep warm in a 200F oven on a parchment-lined pan.

Repeat until all gyoza are cooked, adding more oil to the skillet only as needed.

TO SERVE: Put three gyoza on each individual plate and accompany with little dishes of teriyaki sauce and sweet chile sauce for dipping.

SERVES 10

CUBANS

The first Cubans to leave their island home for the shores of Lake Michigan arrived in the 1950s. This group, numbering approximately 2,000, sought to escape the government of Fulgencio Batista. When Fidel Castro and his Socialist revolution transformed Cuba into a Soviet-like state in 1959, the number of Cuban political refugees rose markedly during the ensuing years.

Between 1960 and 1963, thousands of Cubans, mostly of European descent, made their home in Chicago. This group was almost exclusively comprised of professionals, including doctors, lawyers, dentists, engineers, accountants and teachers. The next "Freedom Flight" wave, coming between 1965 and 1973, brought approximately 20,000 Cubans to Chicago, mostly family members of the earlier arriving professionals. After 1973, Cuban immigration decreased significantly due to the implementation of restrictive federal immigration laws.

Consequently, the next two waves to Chicago did not come by standard channels. The first came in 1980 by way of "The Mariel Boatlift" when Fidel Castro selected groups of mostly poor and single men (many of whom he and his regime deemed "undesirable") to be sent by boat to the shores of America. Sadly, most of these "Mariel" arrivals had

no relatives in Chicago and had to start life anew.

The most recent wave, the *balseros* (boat people), was made up of individuals who lived in conditions of such economic deprivation in Cuba that they were willing to risk their lives to cross the sea to America, often in vessels not seaworthy, for the chance at a better life. For a number of years in the 1990s, the United States Coast Guard rescued these individuals and transported them to the U.S. By 1996, approximately 2,000 *balseros* had settled in Chicago.

Due to a change in federal law, the U.S. Coast Guard is not authorized to transport Cuban nationals to the United States. Under this new law, informally known as the "Dry Land Law," Cuban nationals who reach American soil will be accepted into the United States as a refugee, but any Cuban national found at sea must be escorted back to Cuba. This law is controversial among Cuban Americans as it makes the existence or non-existence of legal refugee status for Cubans turn upon arbitrary circumstances. More importantly, many Cuban Americans fear that the law leaves a Cuban escorted back to Cuba vulnerable to retribution from the Castro regime.

During the 50 years of Cuban settlement in Chicago, this Caribbean community has met

with outstanding success in making its economic, cultural, social and political mark on the Windy City. Of all the Latino communities to call Chicago home, Cubans are the most likely to own their own businesses and residences, often living in the city's most affluent neighborhoods. Cubans own not only food markets, jewelry and clothing shops, but also investment and marketing firms, real estate and insurance brokerages, and construction companies. Moreover, within the vital Cuban business community exists a culture of social advancement, as Cuban women have high participation rates in male-dominated fields such as medicine, law, dentistry and education, including university faculties.

As such, it is not surprising that the Chicago-based Cuban American Chamber of Commerce not only counts over 180 companies among its membership, but also manages a well-financed Chicagoland credit union. In addition, every January 28th it sponsors patriotic celebrations commemorating Cuba's independence from Spain. The date of January 28th is significant as it is the birthday of Jose Martí, who gave his life fighting for Cuba's freedom in the Cuban War of Independence (1895-1898).

The Cuban arrivals to Chicago brought many

Owner Manuel Santiago, Jr. of Cafe Marianao, enjoying an always popular Cuban sandwich at his location on Milwakee Avenue.

Photographer Luis Cabrera enjoying his morning Cafe Cubano at El Rinconcito Cubano. Luis of Face Photo provided all the excellent images used in the Cuban (except for Sacred Heart) and Puerto Rican sections of this publication.

Sacred Heart Catholic Church

faiths with them, including Baptist, Methodist, Pentecostal and Santeria (a synthesis of Catholicism and African religions). However, the vast majority of Chicago's Cubans are Roman Catholics. The power and beauty of their faith can be especially felt on September 8th, the feast of Our Lady of Charity, the patron saint of Cuba. Traditional centers of celebration include Saint Ita in Chicago, Saint Lambert in Skokie, and Sacred Heart in Melrose Park.

Finally, no discussion of the Cuban community would be complete without a nod to the political dynamics still very much at work within this group. Indeed, since the foundations of this community are built upon thousands of personal stories of political exile, the fate of their homeland is still at the forefront of common concern. The Chicago Cuban Americans foresee a Cuba that is more free and prosperous than the one of today. Many Chicago branches of Miami-based political organizations allow Chicago Cubans to work towards that end.

Though no one knows what the future holds for this island state in the next decade, the future of the community from the tropics, which made the often chilly Windy City their thriving home, seems quite bright for years to come.

Owner Nino Rogelo relaxes outside his establishment on Fullerton.

Carlos Laguardia, owner of Cafe Laguardia in Bucktown (Armitage Avenue), serves Jahaira Rodriguez an order of Cuban Nachos.

A tornado destroyed the German 1891 Sacred Heart Church. A new facility in Melrose Park was built in the 1950s. The parish welcomed Cuban refugees in the 1960s and 150 or more of them come back every September 8th to give thanks before their shrine to Our Lady of Charity.

A touch of the "old country" at Cafe Laguardia.

Mr. Sanchez makes one of the famous and fabulous Cuban coffees at Cafe Marianao.

27

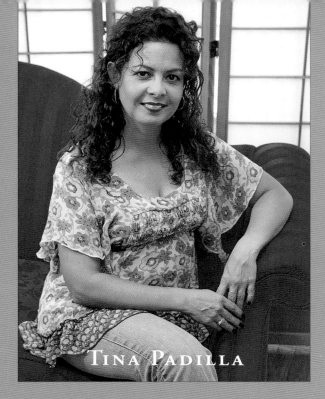

TINA PADILLA

During the early years when I was married, I watched Juanita Gonzalez, my husband's mother, prepare many dishes. Moving from Cuba to Chicago in 1969 to escape the communist dictatorship of Fidel Castro, she told me how ajiaco was the only meal her mother was able to find during the Spanish and Cuban revolutions. It was eaten by Cuban soldiers and the locals so it was considered a "peasant" food.

Though I am a Mexican American Christian, I see myself as a blend of many nationalities: Cuban, Jewish, Japanese, Lebanese, German, Puerto Rican, Italian and African American since these are the cultures that have been fused into the family through my brother's and sister's marriages. Ajiaco is also a fusion of nationalities since the variety of roots hail from Africa, the recipe is Cuban and I add my own Mexican flair. When Juanita moved to Florida, I was mandated to continue the tradition of having ajiaco at Padilla family gatherings and holidays. I love cooking and hope my family and friends enjoy the food I prepare. Ajiaco is, undoubtably, a fantastic fusion of flavors.

28

AJIACO

INGREDIENTS

Vegetables: yuca, calabaza, malanga and yautia, cut into 4 1-inch cubes (possible to increase to 6 2-inch chunks, depending on the size of pot)

(Optional: You may like to add other roots such as ñame, yautia lila and boniato)

2 corn on the cob, cut into thirds

1 ripe plantain, cut into 2-inch sections

BROTH

1 lb. boneless beef or pork, cubed

½ lb. neck bones, beef or pork

(For the vegetarian version omit the beef or pork and substitute a vegetable broth)

1 tbsp. salt

½ tsp. black pepper

3 quarts water

SAUCE

2 tbsp. olive oil

1 tsp. garlic powder (or 5 fresh garlic cloves, minced or pressed)

1 tbsp. adobo (a Latin all-purpose seasoning)

1 envelope of sazon

4 tbsp. of sofrito

1 can tomato sauce

½ cup red wine

GARNISH

½ head iceberg lettuce, shredded

Cilantro, chopped

2 limes, sliced

1 jalapeno, chopped

Avocado

Sour cream

Peel and cube fresh vegetables, then set aside with corn and plantain. To make broth, add boneless beef or pork, neck bones, black pepper, salt and three quarts water to a very large pot. Cook for one hour. Meanwhile, preheat skillet to make sauce, then add olive oil and fry garlic. Stir in remaining seasonings, tomato sauce and wine, then simmer for ten minutes.

Once the meat is fully cooked, remove the neck bones and meat. You might want to leave some meat in though I prefer to use just the broth. Add all fresh vegetables and prepared sauce to the broth. Cover and cook on moderate heat for 20-30 minutes until vegetables soften. Garnish.

SERVES 6-8

GERMAN

People from German-speaking lands had been consistently crossing the Atlantic to settle in America since long before the Revolutionary War, but their numbers could only be deemed moderate. It was not until the tumultuous revolutionary period of the decades following the final defeat of Napoleon Bonaparte in 1815, that Germans began to migrate in waves. Indeed, between 1820 and 1930, 5.9 million Germans arrived in the United States, their influence touching every region of the country, but especially the Midwest, which was similar in topographical and climatic conditions to Germany. As such, cities like Milwaukee, St. Louis, Cincinnati, Cleveland, and, of course, Chicago, would become home to large German populations.

As if by some turn of fate, not unlike the set destinies found in so many Germanic tales of old, the fortunes of the German immigrant and of the young City of Chicago met in the first half of the 19th century, and then rose meteorically, on parallel, but complementary paths well into the 20th century.

Some Germans emigrated for reasons of religious freedom, but most left on the basis of political and economic factors. Not even a united nation until 1870, the 19th century was a time of overpopulation, scarcity of resources and economic stagnation for the German territories. A late arrival of the Industrial Revolution only exacerbated the distress, while German inheritance laws, by allowing for partial inheritance, caused many German males to inherit parcels of land that were too small to sustain a family.

During the 1830s and '40s, the fertile lands of the American Great Plains opened for settlement. The prospect of large farms of black soil upon which no noble had a prior claim was appealing enough to convince millions of Germans to cross the ocean. The first major influx arrived in Chicago just as the city was coming to life. While some used the city as a temporary home, a place to earn money before moving west, many, especially those with skills in demand, concluded their journey in Chicago. Some of these new German immigrants were university educated or accomplished tradesmen, many having fled the 1848 Revolution in the German states after having supported the wrong side. A later study of the educational and trade backgrounds of Chicago's early German immigrants confirmed that almost 62% were professionals, white-collar workers, or skilled craftsmen. These advantages helped this group to quickly establish themselves in the local brewing, malting, baking and confectionery trades, and further, to successfully conduct business in English-speaking Chicago soon after their arrival.

As early as 1850, one-sixth of Chicago was German, and by 1900, a full one-fourth of Chicagoans, 470,000 strong, claimed German ancestry. Chicago's German immigrants originated from all over the German states, with roughly 55% of them hailing from Roman Catholic backgrounds, less than 5% from Jewish backgrounds, and the rest, Protestant. Once settled into Chicago, the Germans built an impressive network of religious, social, educational, political and leisure institutions, which addressed every German need, ranging from Turner (athletic) organizations where heated political discussions often erupted, to relaxing Sundays at a brewery-sponsored *biergarten*.

Yet the Germans were not a uniform group. Walls of class, religion, politics and regional background divided them just as they had in the Old Country. In addition, over time, the immigration experience itself introduced a new wall; that of the time of arrival. By 1900, the original immigrating generation of the 1830s and '40s and their children lived comfortably within the German network of activities and organizations. Many offspring had little first-hand memory of Germany, but most had economic security in the artisan niches carved out by their parents.

All captions in the German chapter are by Bob Skilnik.

Chicago's turn-of-the-century German-owned saloons offered something for almost everyone. The boarding house above this saloon could just as well housed a meeting place for political or union organizations responsive to German American interests.

The next group, having arrived as part of the third wave of immigration beginning in the 1880s, possessed a solid connection to Germany, and thus infused a stronger sense of the German *geist* (spirit) into their community. This group tended to own small businesses that catered to Germans. The tail end of this wave arrived in the 1890s, when Germany had industrialized, thereby bringing a memory of a Germany very different than that of earlier arrivals.

Class divisions could also be felt in every part of German Chicago. Middle-class and working-class Germans attended parallel, but separate clubs. Although both classes celebrated *Karneval* and held Christmas bazaars, the working-class festivals often included a political speech or demonstration. Moreover, though 1900 saw a strong German middle class and burgeoning elite, the two-thirds of Germans who still found themselves among the working class were exposed to theories of Socialism and the more extreme Marxism. As a result, members of the politicized German working class founded and participated in workers' associations and unions in great numbers. Indeed, many Chicago Germans created organizational structures that would be used as the basis of the national and international labor movements of the 20th century.

But despite internal divisions, nearly all Germans were united on three issues: the proliferation of a strong press, the preservation

Chicago History Museum

of the German language and the safeguarding of German leisure culture.

By the turn of the 19th century, a powerful German-language press was firmly in place, as represented by the Illinois *Staats-Zeitung*, the *Chicagoer Arbeiter-Zeitung*, the Chicago *Freie Presse* and the *Abendpost*. Each strongly advocated the preservation of the German language. Starting in the 1860s, the Chicago Public Schools began teaching German. However, when school budgets tightened, German was often the first subject to go. As such, until World War I, Germans had to be highly cognizant of school board elections and mobilized votes for German-friendly officials.

Finally, Germans of all classes, faiths and backgrounds cherished weekend celebrations with family and friends where lager beer was the drink of choice. This *biergarten* culture collided with turn-of-the-century temperance and religious movements, often spearheaded by strict, middle-class Protestants whose families had been in America for several generations. The temperance movement led to laws that restricted the sale of alcohol and required businesses to be closed on Sundays. German Chicagoans vehemently opposed these laws, as they forcibly eliminated traditional German American activities, especially the Sunday opening of Chicago saloons for working-class Germans, who usually had only Sunday off work.

This suppression of the *biergarten* culture was a harbinger of things to come. The network of German clubs, organizations, newspapers and language instruction went into hiding when the United States entered World War I in opposition to Germany, and all but disappeared with the coming of World War II. After two generations of Americanization in the face of two world wars and the atrocities committed by the German state in World War II, many German Chicagoans had distanced themselves from German-speaking Chicago.

Though the days of German in every public school classroom will never return, currently German tradition is awaking anew, its revival most apparent during Oktoberfest when every Chicagoan seems to claim a link to German heritage, especially over a second or third *stein* of German beer.

While their men enjoyed a weekend "hunt," these "hausfrauen" (housewives) share gossip in the pleasure of a neighborhood Kaffee Klatsch.

Chicago History Museum

Judging from the "game" in front of these smiling members of a local "jaegerverein" (hunting club), they've bagged their limit for the day.

Chicago History Museum

A proud "fräulein" (young lady) waves to the crowd.

Phineas Jones

Typical of many of Chicago's early "tied house" saloons, the rounded metal signage and the advertising above the entrance indicate that this establishment was controlled (tied) by the Conrad Seipp Brewing Company, one of the city's largest Pre-Prohibition German-owned breweries.

Chicago History Museu

Sean Benham

Sean Benham

Phineas Jone

The annual Von Steuben Parade is the German American event of the year when hundreds of participants march, dance, play music or ride the many beautiful floats on Lincoln

BISTRO-STYLE LAMB SHANK

INGREDIENTS

3 tbsp. olive oil

8–10 12-oz. lamb shanks

Salt and cracked black pepper

½ cup white onions, diced

½ cup celery, diced

½ cup carrots, diced

1 tbsp. garlic, chopped

1 cup white wine

4 cups tomato purée

2 bay leaves

1 sprig fresh rosemary (plus extra for garnish)

1-2 cups chicken or veal broth

¾ cup dry sherry

3 tbsp. cornstarch slurry (made by mixing equal amounts cornstarch and cold water)

1 14-oz. can cannelloni beans, rinsed and drained

Salt and ground black pepper (for adjusting seasoning)

2 cups fresh plum tomatoes, diced

½ cup parsley, minced

¾ cup scallions, chopped

In large roasting pot, heat oil on high until smoking. Season lamb shanks with salt and cracked black pepper. Brown on all sides; remove lamb and set aside. Do not clean the pot.

In the same pot, place onions, celery, carrots and garlic; sauté for 3 minutes. Add wine to deglaze the pan then reduce wine by two-thirds. Add in meat. Add tomato purée, bay leaves, rosemary sprig and enough broth to cover the meat; bring to a boil. Cover and place in oven for 1½ to 2 hours, or until meat is 165 degrees and tender.

Remove lamb from pan and keep warm until ready to serve. Remove and discard rosemary sprig and bay leaves. Add sherry to sauce and thicken with cornstarch slurry. Bring to a boil, whisking constantly. Decrease heat and stir in cannelloni beans, cooking just long enough to heat them through. Adjust seasonings. Stir in diced plum tomatoes, parsley and chopped scallions.

To serve, place a lamb shank on each individual dinner or soup plate and top with one cup of sauce.

SERVES 8

CARLYN BERGHOFF

I have been living the American Dream, thanks to the initiative of my great-grandfather who came to the United States to start a small brewery. He experienced many setbacks, beginning with a fire in his brewery in Fort Wayne, Indiana as well as being barred from setting up his business at the 1893 World's Fair in Chicago.

Not deterred, he opened a booth outside of the fairgrounds and sold his German-style beer. His entrepreneurial spirit motivated him to successfully open a saloon at the corner of State and Adams streets where he sold his beer and a wide variety of sandwiches.

Throughout the following generations, my family carried forth his entrepreneurial spirit with the development of new menu items and additional locations. Many of the selections from the menu came from family

recipes. The hearty, comforting lamb shank was one of my mother's favorites and has been a featured item ever since it first appeared on The Berghoff menu in 1918.

"Tradition with a twist" was my mission when I opened The Berghoff in Chicago.

Our cuisine is a blend of German and European, complemented by farm-fresh local ingredients and with contemporary presentation. Located in the lower level of the historic Berghoff Building on 17 West Adams, Berghoff Beer and Root Beer are steady staples of The Berghoff.

I am proud and blessed to enjoy a rich family heritage. Providing a legendary dining experience for the great City of Chicago is an added bonus in our own version of living the American Dream.

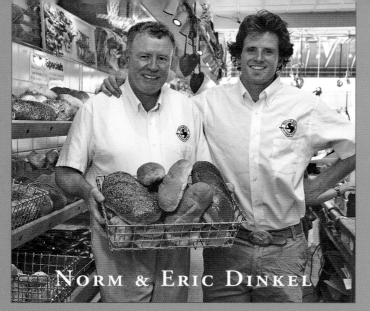

NORM & ERIC DINKEL

ALMOND SPRITZ COOKIES

INGREDIENTS

1.6 oz. (¼ cup) almond paste

6.4 oz. (9/10 cup) granulated sugar

8 oz. (1⅛ cup) butter

1 egg

1.4 oz. (1/5 cup) milk

1/2 tsp. almond (or 1 tsp. vanilla) extract

12.8 oz. (3 cups) pastry or all-purpose flour

Preheat oven to 365 degrees. With an electric mixer, beat almond paste, granulated sugar and butter until smooth. Add egg, milk and almond (or vanilla) extract and beat until smooth. Add flour then beat at low-speed for 1-2 minutes. Bag out dough using a decorative disc (or spoon) one-inch apart on parchment paper or on lightly greased baking pans. Sprinkle with granulated sugar. Bake 12-15 minutes until edges are golden. Let cool. These cookies will keep fresh or frozen if packed tightly.

SERVES 12-15

Growing up in a family bakery means that you learn how to bake and wear many hats. My great-grandfather, Joseph K., was a master baker in Bavaria, Germany. Coming to America in 1900, he and his wife, Antonie, eventually moved to Chicago and founded Dinkel's Bakery in 1922. It started out with Antonie selling and managing in the front of the store while Joseph toiled in the back.

The bakery business has been a real family affair. In 1932, my grandfather, Norman J., joined the business and, in 1972, my father Norman, Jr. (photo above, at left) officially took the helm. Our neighborhood on North Lincoln Avenue has changed many times as the Germans began assimilating and moving further out. In the early 1980s, our store was one of the few left open on the entire block. Currently our neighborhood, once again, has revived and we are back in full swing. We love being part of Chicago's German heritage, one of the city's vital cornerstones. We are proud of our achievements and contribution to the community.

Our almond spritz cookie is a recipe my grandfather, Norman, Sr., introduced during our 50th anniversary celebration.

Though I am officially not at the helm of Dinkel's Bakery, I have worked here on and off my entire life. I love the tradition of the bakery and the feeling of a delicious baked strudel or stollen in my belly!

RIND ROLLADEN (BEEF ROLLUPS)

INGREDIENTS

4 thin-sliced round steaks (a maximum of
⅛-inch thick)

16 strips raw bacon

1 medium yellow onion, coarsely chopped

Processed dill pickles (not the fresh, deli-
styled), cut into quartered spears

8 tbsp. yellow mustard, divided

8.5 oz. ground horseradish

2 cups flour

1 quart beef bouillon

Water, as needed

1 cup dry vermouth

Salt

Pepper

Toothpicks or kitchen string

4 tbsp. cooking oil (olive or peanut)

Maggi (or Worcestershire) sauce to taste

Cornstarch

Cut each round steak vertically along the muscle separation. Trim fat. Using a meat mallet, lightly pound each piece of meat. Season each steak with a generous pinch of salt and pepper. Coat one side of each steak with at least two tablespoons of yellow mustard. Now coat steaks with one tablespoon horseradish. Place two strips of bacon parallel to each other, longways on top of the coated steak. Lay one pickle spear horizontally at one end of steak, tuck in sides if possible and roll steak like a burrito. Take at least two toothpicks and secure rolled meat together. Place assembled rolladen on a platter.

Dredge rolladen in flour. Add three tablespoons oil to a 12-inch frying pan then heat oil at medium high until it begins to shimmer. Brown rolladen on all sides, being careful not to loosen toothpicks (about ten minutes).

Once browned, remove rolladen and carefully place into a deep pot, which accommodates layering.

Add one tablespoon of oil to original frying pan. Add chopped onion and fry in steak drippings until the onion becomes translucent. Using a slotted spoon, remove onions and spread over rolladen. Pour one cup of vermouth into frying pan. Stir and scrape to loosen any flour and bits of meat on the bottom of the pan. Pour vermouth mixture into pot.

Pour bouillon into pot and add water if necessary, enough to cover rolladen. If you have any horseradish left, add it to the pot. Bring liquid to a boil and then turn down heat to a high simmer. Cook two hours or until beef is very tender.

Carefully remove rolladen from pot with slotted spoon. Skim fat. Reheat liquid until boiling and add cornstarch/water paste. Stir until gravy thickens and check for seasoning, adding a tablespoon of Maggi and/or salt and pepper, if desired. Add rolladen back into the gravy, heat through and serve with gravy. Recommended side servings are boiled red potatoes or egg noodles and red cabbage.

SERVES 8

BOB SKILNIK

I was born into a family which was first-generation American. My paternal grandfather came to the U.S. from Germany and my mother's family, pure Irish folks, arrived in America prior to the Civil War.

Drawing upon his heritage, my father loved cooking German dishes, and his joy inspired a culinary interest in me. My family still enjoys a variety of German meals (many from his recipes), and one of our favorites is rind rolladen, which is a beef rollup similar to "braciolone," an entrée from Italy. The dish probably finds its roots in Bavaria in Southern Germany, where beef was readily available, as the majority of Germany's cattle grazed in the foothills of the Alps.

My father often made a beef rollup using carrots, bacon and a bit of onion as stuffing, while boosting the gravy with the addition of a 12-ounce can of light-bodied beer from a neighborhood brewery. His rollup was delicious! With my recipe, I took the basic ingredients and substituted vermouth for the beer. In addition, I discovered that 8 ounces of the sweeter German Fest, Marezen, or Octoberfest-styled beers can be substituted for the vermouth, providing an even sweeter-tasting gravy. In a pinch, the Mexican beer, Negra Modelo, can also produce similar results.

Without question, cooking is one of my favorite pastimes, along with writing and studying world history. But when I take my rind rolladen out of the oven, it's time to sit down and savor this fabulous dish.

GREEK

The story of the Greeks in Chicago demonstrates that hard work, attempting new occupations, and giving support to fellow countrymen will translate into success, even in a strange, new world.

During the 1840s, the first Greeks to reach Chicago were a group of mostly sailors who traveled the commercial routes from New Orleans to the Great Lakes via the Mississippi and Illinois rivers. Born in a world of rugged hills and seemingly a thousand islands, these men tasted the sea with their first breath, and they were nurtured to manhood under a warm, Mediterranean sun. Thus, the first winter in a flat, prairie-encircled Chicago of biting winds and heavy snows must have proven memorably foreign. Yet, these men did not shy away from the challenge. Instead, they saw what was wonderful in the city and sung its praises to their countrymen back in Greece. Those early seamen set the pattern for the Greeks who would follow: for the Greek immigrants never forgot their homeland, traditions and faith, but upon disembarking in flat, lake-bordered Chicago, they fearlessly faced a new future.

It was not until Chicago needed to be built anew, after the Great Fire of 1871, that the Greeks came in great numbers. Men arrived first. Most came from the Peloponnesus (the southern

The water tower on Michigan Avenue was one of the few structures to survive the Great Fire of 1871.

peninsula of Greece), in particular, the provinces of Sparta, Arcadia and Laconia; and from families who had engaged in grazing or agricultural pursuits for centuries. However, upon landing in Chicago, these men tackled urban life by becoming produce peddlers on Lake, Randolph and South Water streets and acquiring construction jobs rebuilding the city.

One of the early immigrants, Christ Chakonas, who arrived to Chicago from Sparta in 1872, became so excited at the economic opportunities that he repeatedly traveled back and forth from Sparta to persuade other Greek men to immigrate. For his efforts, Chakonas was called the "Columbus of Sparta."

Chakonas' task was made easier by the terrible constellation of troubles that plagued 19th century Greece. Originally united under Alexander the Great in 336 B.C., this home of the political theory of democracy and of the foundations of Western philosophy, would eventually fall under the control of the Roman Empire, which in turn was profoundly influenced by Greek culture and thought. In 330 A.D. the Roman Empire split into Western and Eastern halves, with Greece in the Eastern Empire. After the fall of the Western Empire in the 5th century, the Eastern (or Byzantine) Empire was centered in Constantinople (present-day Istanbul) and remained a prosperous center for civilization for another millennium. But when Constantinople fell to the Ottoman Turks, so too did Greece, leaving the entire country subject to wretched foreign occupation for almost 400 years. In 1821, Greece achieved independence for part of its territory, while the rest remained under

The Zaganos family immigrated to America in 1907.

Circa 1930. Greek Chicagoans set up spits in back alleys to roast several lambs in one sitting.

After the Chicago Fire in 1871, Greeks came to America to help rebuild the city.

George and Margie Poulos opened Margie's Candy and Ice Cream Shop on Western Avenue in 1921.

41

Ottoman control. By the 19th century, much of the country, Ottoman or independent, was caught in the vice of severe poverty and economic depression. High unemployment reigned, while property prices steadily rose. At the same time, the agricultural class, the group from which most Chicago Greeks originated, faced a perfect storm of drought, crop failures, falling crop prices and soil deterioration. As a result, many families were left deeply in debt. To make matters worse, for that portion of Greece under Ottoman control, Ottoman law mandated that the male residents of occupied Greece be subject to military conscription. As such, many men from those lands eagerly crossed the Atlantic to avoid conscription in the Turkish army.

However, despite the serious economic and political burdens imposed upon their homeland, the vast majority of Greek men who immigrated after the 1871 Chicago Fire planned to return home eventually. They hoped the economic opportunities of Chicago would allow them to earn enough to support families at home, to fund dowries for sisters and daughters and to extinguish family debts. Many Greeks achieved this goal, as shown by the fact that approximately 40% of the Greeks who had come to the United States prior to 1940 had returned to Greece.

As for the other 60%, circumstances or change of heart kept them in America. Prior to World War II, Chicago was home to more Greeks than any other American city.

The decision to settle brought with it the desire for family. Thus, Greek women, slowly, but surely, would follow their countrymen to Chicago. The first Greek woman came to Chicago in 1885. However, not until after the turn of the century did Greek women arrive in great numbers. Most of the women who entered Chicago in the early 1900s were "picture brides," meaning that the couple became engaged before ever laying eyes on one another, with the would-be husband deciding on his future bride on the basis of a photograph and whatever information had been imparted to him. Once in Chicago, these women generally held to Greek social tradition and did not work outside the home.

During the first few decades of the 20th century, the Greeks moved beyond produce peddling and achieved great success in more sophisticated mercantile ventures, such as restaurants, florist shops and ice cream production. Indeed, despite the fact that the vast majority of these immigrants came from rural backgrounds, by 1927 more than 10,000 Chicago-area stores were owned and run by Greeks, with these establishments earning $2 million dollars per day.

The community settled on the Near West Side in the geographical triangle formed by Blue Island, Halsted, Harrison and Polk streets. This neighborhood became known as the "Greek Delta" or as "Greektown." Fused together by language and the Greek Orthodox religion, the Greektown community became especially tight and self-contained. This was, in part, due to the fact that the multi-ethnic intermarriage possibilities that one would find with, for example, followers of the Catholic faith did not exist to the same extent for Greek Orthodox adherents. Moreover, having originated from a land in which islands, steep hills and rough terrain created natural barriers between villages and settlements,

Sianis Family

Bill Sianis and his Billy Goat with guests at his Billy Goat Tavern on North Michigan Avenue.

Parthenon Restaurant

Opaa!
Flaming saganaki.

Panos Fiorentinos

Annunciation
Greek Orthodox Church was
built in 1914 on LaSalle Street.

42

the Greeks had a long cultural history of relying on family, clansmen and fellow villagers to sustain themselves in isolated locations. Thus, in this small area, the Greek immigrants seemingly created their own little nation with churches, schools, shops, restaurants, Greek doctors and lawyers, businesses, ethnic societies and Greek-language newspapers. This self-sufficient community, with its stunning churches, such as Holy Trinity Greek Orthodox, founded in Greektown in 1897, and its Greek schools, which passed on the Greek language to following generations, is testimony to the fact that though Greek Chicagoans might be willing to stay in America and make their living in occupations never imagined by their grandfathers, they would never forget their native homeland and heritage.

Yet the Greek immigrants embraced their new American home by learning English and becoming educated about the American Republic. More than any other Chicagoan, social reformer Jane Addams was instrumental in helping the Greek immigrant adapt. Her Hull House, located in the area of the Greek Delta, did not only provide language instruction and social service assistance. It was also a place of joy; full of activities, sports and theatrical productions, including ancient Greek dramas. For the Greek Chicagoans, it became a second home. In 1935, when the hearse for Jane Addams passed, Greektown stood silently in respect for their "Saint of Halsted Street."

The end of World War II brought a new wave of Greek immigrants to Chicago. Most entered the United States as displaced persons since Greece had suffered under Nazi occupation and had endured severe political turmoil in the years following. As was the norm, the new Greek arrivals brought new life to Greektown.

Yet the time of the old self-contained Greektown was soon to pass, as much of the land that was Greektown became the campus of the University of Illinois at Chicago. Simultaneously, other large sections were sliced off by the construction of the Eisenhower and Kennedy Expressways. A multi-ethnic group of neighborhood activists fought to save the Delta area scheduled for destruction. The Supreme Court of the United States summarily ended their battle when it decided in favor of the developers. Area residents were given little compensation for their homes and one year to move. For this reason, along with suburban expansion and the building of Greek Orthodox churches outside the city limits, Greektown residents dispersed and moved to other city neighborhoods and suburbs.

However, just as Greektown was being changed forever, yet another wave of Greek immigration began after the repeal of the 1965 National Origins Act, which had imposed restrictions on Greek immigration. Since that time, as many as 260,000 Greeks have come to America.

As of the 2000 census, 93,140 Greek Americans lived in the Chicagoland area. The group is still dominant in mercantile enterprises, and a great many Greek Chicagoans populate the affluent professional class of the city. But this success has not necessitated a loss of cultural memory. Greek Orthodox priests still serve large congregations, Greek American children pursue the Greek language and Chicagoans of every background still delight in the delicious delicacies of the restaurants of Greektown.

A Greek-inspired monument at the southeast corner of Monroe and Halsted streets.

A Greek dancer in traditional costume.

The annual Taste of Greece is held at the end of August. This festival, always located in Greektown on Halsted Street, celebrates the joy of Hellenic culture and cuisine.

PASTICHIO

INGREDIENTS

3 lbs. ground round steak or
    ground beef

¼ lb. butter

1 can tomato paste

3 eggs

2 onions, chopped finely

1 lb. Greek macaroni (#2) or
    other thick macaroni

1 cup grated cheese (Myzithra or Romano)

1 tsp. cinnamon

1 tsp. nutmeg

Salt and pepper to taste

TOPPING

2 cups milk, heated

¼ cup butter

4 tbsp. flour

4 eggs

1 cup grated cheese

Cinnamon

PASTICHIO: Brown meat in butter. Add tomato paste, chopped onion, salt, pepper, cinnamon and nutmeg. Cook until most of the liquid is absorbed and drain the rest.

Boil macaroni in salt water for nine minutes. Macaroni should be partially cooked. Drain hot macaroni in colander then rinse with cold water and drain again.

Beat three eggs then mix in one cup of grated cheese.

Combine meat, macaroni and egg mixture in large bowl with your hands. Pour macaroni mixture into a well greased 9"x 12" pan.

TOPPING: Melt butter then stir in flour to make a roux. Slowly add heated milk to thicken sauce.

Beat four eggs very well then add two tablespoons grated cheese. Pour into the milk/butter mixture, adding slowly and stirring constantly.

Spinkle remaining cheese over the macaroni in the pan then pour topping evenly over. Sprinkle lightly with cinnamon. Bake in 350 degree oven for 45 minutes until the top is lightly browned.

A dowry was of paramount importance to a Greek family. My dad's mother, Yiayia Helen, was one of eleven children, and her father co-owned a hotel/restaurant in Tripoli, Greece. He sold his partnership and came to America in 1910 to earn money to help pay for the wedding, and the dowry, for each of his six daughters. He initially became a chef in Greektown before opening his own restaurant at Halsted and Harrison.

When my yiayia came to America and married in 1924, she thereafter made pastichio for all of the birthday parties and special celebrations of her loved ones. When I dine in Greektown, I always hope to taste her recipe. Many have come close, but hers is the one I favor most.

Most Greeks don't write down their recipes, but my Aunt Mary pieced together the directions for my yiayia's pastichio and her family passed it down to me.

First served in the larger, city-based areas in Greece like Athens, Sparta and Tripoli, chefs developed the dish to appeal to the tastes of affluent citizens and tourists.

In the United States, pastichio, along with moussaka, gyros, baklava and Greek salad, have come to epitomize traditional Greek cooking.

My book, Greektown Chicago: Its History, Its Recipes (2005), *was a complement to my quest to learn more about the Greeks of Chicago and also enjoy our rich gastronomic heritage.*

The history of Greeks in Chicago goes back to the late 1800s and every time I see the restored Water Tower on Michigan Avenue, I think of how many of my ancestors helped in the construction of the city after the Great Fire. I think of the peddlers who used to ply the streets and alleyways, feeding the workers with fruits and vegetables from their carts. I see the tower in a new light, remembering how Greeks were part of the rebirth of this great city we enjoy today.

See you in Greektown!

ALEXA GANAKOS

MARIA MELIDIS

My husband "Yianni" was my high school sweetheart. We married in 1971 and Kesara, my first child, was born in 1971. Our son, George, was born when we moved to the United States in 1978. Family is important to us and that is what we try to reflect in our Greektown eateries, Pegasus and Artopolis. Everyone who enters is treated like family. We also feel it's important to share with and educate our clientele about the healthy cuisine of Greece, its traditional recipes and heart-stopping landscapes.

Our artopita (town of bread) is a savory pie which provides a connecting thread among many traditional dishes. Bread is important to the Greeks and we like to flavor it. We add fresh garden vegetables, cheeses, and farm-raised meats which elevate bread to a healthy art. Our menu items are so unique, they have their own U.S. government patents.

Coming to Chicago in 1986, we realized that Greek cuisine was represented from only one region and many locals thought that Greeks only eat lamb, moussaka, pastichio and baklava. However, the food of Patras, my hometown on the Peloponnese, was influenced by our Italian neighbors. After World War II when Italian armies arrived in Greece, many soldiers intermarried with Greeks. Since my husband's roots are in both Italy and Asia Minor, the recipes and teachings of my mother-in-law were treasures we brought with us to America.

However, I am first and foremost a wife, mother and grandmother. The "stereoma" (family structure) is what gives Greek heritage its longevity and tremendous feeling of warmth and hospitality.

ARTOPITA

INGREDIENTS

1 lb. spinach leaves, fresh or frozen (thawed)

½ of a leek root

1 white and 1 green onion, chopped thinly

Salt and pepper to taste

2 oz. heavy cream

1 egg, beaten, plus 1 egg beaten

½ lb. Feta cheese

DOUGH

1 lb. Harvest flour

4 oz. Prozymi (cultured starter dough) or 2 envelopes active dry yeast

2 cups lukewarm water

1 tsp. salt

2 lbs. unsalted Plugra (French high-fat butter) or regular unsalted butter

. . . .

Dough: Dissole yeast or prozymi in lukewarm water in mixing bowl. Add flour, salt, cut in butter. Knead slightly and set aside in refrigerator.

Filling: If using frozen spinach; thaw, drain and slice thinly. If using fresh; wash, drain and slice thinly. In a frying pan, sauté onions, leek and spinach. Remove from heat and let mix cool. Mix in heavy cream, egg and Feta then combine well.

Preheat oven to 350 degrees. Roll out pastry dough into two sheets, approximately ¼-inch thick. Take a shallow, ovenproof glass pie plate and brush with oil. Place one sheet of dough into the bottom, covering all sides. Pour in the filling. Cover with the other sheet of dough and tuck in any edges that fall over the sides of the pan. Mix remaining egg with two tablespoons water to make an egg wash. Brush top of pastry with egg wash. Refrigerate until dish cools. Bake for 30-45 minutes or until golden brown.

SERVES 2-4

OLGA PAXINOS

My parents came from Crete. This is my mother's recipe which she prepared for festive occasions. I prefer hers to others because the addition of ouzo and orange juice give it an aromatic taste. When we lost her, my father continued the tradition.

As to my family heritage, my grandfather came to Chicago in 1910 and my father in 1920. He went back to marry my mother in 1931. A shoemaker by trade, my father became a cook here before opening up a little 16-seater called the White Dome Grill at Grand and Clark. A typical Greek family, we spoke Greek at home and all five of us were well-educated.

What do I like best about being Greek in Chicago? It is being a part of a large Greek community, carrying on traditions for my family and the freedom to express our Greek Orthodoxy. For 40 years, we have belonged to St. Spyridon Parish in Palos Heights. Formerly in the Chicago Roseland area, our church recently celebrated its 90th anniversary. Like my mother before me, I love to cook, to bake and watch everyone enjoy my labor of love.

XEROTIGANA
(SYRUP-DIPPED SPIRAL PASTRY)

INGREDIENTS

3 large eggs

8 oz. freshly squeezed orange juice

3 oz. corn oil

Pinch of salt

2 oz. ouzo (or Masticha liqueur)

All-purpose flour, enough to make a
    soft dough (3-4 cups)

Corn oil for deep frying

2 cups chopped walnuts

SYRUP:

5 cups sugar

3 cups water

1 stick cinnamon

6 cloves

Juice of one lemon

Beat eggs with whisk. Add other liquid ingredients and salt. Slowly add flour, beating until it requires hands to mix. Keep adding flour and mix with hands until dough is soft and not too sticky. Knead dough on counter for about 5-7 minutes. Let dough rest, covered for 30 minutes. Divide into six balls. Flour surface and dough. With rolling pin, roll out one ball at a time into a thin circle. Using an edged pastry cutter, cut into one-inch strips. Take strip and wrap loosely around hand a few times, stretching the dough a little. Secure with two toothpicks. Carefully drop into 350-degree corn oil, using two forks to keep dough circular. Do not fry more than two at a time. Turn xerotigana over in oil a few times. Fry until they turn a light brown. Drain on paper towel, remove toothpicks, dip into cooled syrup for a minute and sprinkle with chopped nuts. Finish all the strips and begin with next dough ball.

Syrup: Bring sugar, water, cloves and cinnamon to a boil. Boil for 20 minutes; add the lemon juice and boil a few more minutes. Allow to cool.

SERVES 60

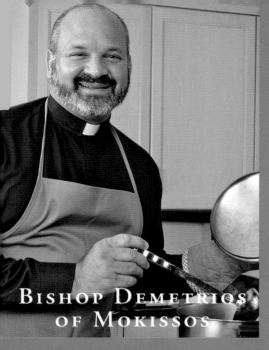

BISHOP DEMETRIOS OF MOKISSOS

A native Chicagoan, I first received my graduate divinity degree from Hellenic College and Holy Cross School of Theology in Brookline, Massachusetts in 1987, and then pursued a doctoral philosophy program at Chicago's Loyola University. In 1992, I was ordained to the priesthood and elevated in 1995 to the rank of Archimandrite, all through the hands of the now Metropolitan Iakovos of Chicago—a long way from the junior altar boy who pedaled to church while his family still slept!

Recently I was elected an Assistant Bishop to the Archdiocese of America by the Holy and Sacred Synod of the Ecumenical Patriarchate and ordained the title of the once renowned diocese of Mokissos. I continue to serve the needs of Greek Orthodox Christians of the Metropolis of Chicago as Chancellor and now Bishop.

As a writer, I have contributed regularly to editorials about issues concerning the Greek Orthodox Faith and Hellenic culture. I co-founded an initiative to improve relations between the Turkish and Greek communities. But hard work and initiative does not stop there as I am also a connoisseur of good food and great soups.

"Avgolemono" (egg-lemon) soup hails from mainland Greece and is considered a "farmer's soup," which is another name for it. A Greek can walk to the garden and pick a lemon from the tree, gather eggs, fetch a chicken from the yard, then go to the market to find the "orzo" (rice). In Chicago, this can prove to be a challenge. However, I managed to find a way to echo the flavors of Greek farms and fields with a recipe that sings of my roots as well as my family's roots in Greece.

According to Epicurus, it is important to "live well and enjoy the simple things in life." Add to that hard work, compassion and gusto.

50

AVGOLEMONO
(EGG LEMON SOUP)

INGREDIENTS

½ of a chicken (with skin)

3 organic lemons, large (room temperature)

3 eggs, large (room temperature)

48 oz. College Inn chicken broth

1½ cups Uncle Ben's converted rice (more if you desire
    thicker soup, add less for thinner soup)

1 tsp. pepper

1 tsp. salt

. . . .

Combine chicken, salt, pepper, and three quarts of water into large pot. Bring the chicken to a boil covered, then cover askew to reduce the broth a bit. Simmer until the meat starts to fall off the bone, approximately one hour. Skim the froth off the boiling water and dispose. Let the chicken cool then skin and de-bone.

Put College Inn chicken broth into pot with existing broth and bring to a boil. Add rice and boil covered for 20 minutes (longer for softer rice). Crack eggs into a separate bowl. Roll lemons firmly on the counter to soften up the lemon to provide more juice. Squeeze lemon juice from three lemons and combine with three whole eggs to blend. Cut up chicken thoroughly.

While constantly stirring eggs and lemon, add the broth slowly—a ladle at a time—while at the same time kissing the air (this seemingly benign action of kissing the air will keep the mixture from curdling, according to grandmother).

Pour the egg-lemon broth mixture back into the pot with the rice and add the chicken. Salt and pepper to taste. Add more lemon if desired.

SERVES 6–8

IRISH

The story of the Irish in Chicago provides dramatic evidence for the power of human potential when given freedom and the opportunity to prove oneself unencumbered. For when the Irish arrived on the shores of Lake Michigan during the 19th and early 20th centuries, most had never known a day free from oppression, as Ireland had been under English occupation for many centuries. However, once in Chicago, the Irish blossomed into a brilliantly dynamic group that has left its lasting mark on the City of Chicago. Indeed, not only did these immigrants work for Ireland's independence, but their determination helped many of them rise to places of prominence in politics, government, education, trade unions, social services, journalism,

law and the Roman Catholic Church.

A flourishing Celtic society during the early centuries of the first millennium A.D., Ireland converted to Christianity in the 5th century due to the efforts of St. Patrick and other early missionaries. The combined introduction of the tenets of the new faith and the Latin alphabet sparked a cultural and intellectual Renaissance on the island. While much of Western Europe fell into a chaos in the wake of the crumbling of the Roman Empire, the Irish lived in a thriving, uniquely Celtic Catholic world in which codified *Brehon* (Gaelic) laws kept order and seemingly a thousand monasteries dotted the landscape. In those monasteries Irish monks and nuns preserved not only the teachings

of the Bible and early Church theologians, but also the knowledge of the ancient world on gorgeous, illuminated manuscripts. Further, many of these Irish religious ventured out into the world as missionaries, converting many peoples throughout Western and Central Europe.

However, this "golden age" of Gaelic society began to wane as the English began their encroachment into Ireland during the 12th century. Over the next few centuries the Irish became increasingly more subject to the demands of the English crown. However, with the coming of the English Reformation, the fortunes of the Irish plummeted dramatically, as the vast majority of the Irish chose to remain Roman Catholic. In an

52

effort to stamp out this loyalty to Catholicism, the English not only transplanted thousands of English and Scottish Protestants to the island, but also took control over the island, thereby stripping the Irish of their land and their rights. By the 18th and early 19th centuries, life for the Irish had reached a new low. Moreover, until the early 19th century, the practicing of Roman Catholicism (the religion of the vast majority of the island) was illegal.

Because of land restrictions most Catholic families only had very small parcels to farm. Moreover, because the Penal Laws mandated partial inheritance, these small parcels grew ever smaller. Thus, many Irish farmers lived at a subsistence level, with potatoes constituting the main food staple. When a fungus attacked the potato crop of Irish farmers in 1845 and for five concurrent harvests thereafter, the English government decided not to import food to the island. As a result, over 1 million people died of starvation and disease, while 1.5 million emigrated out of Ireland during the next 80 years. The famine led to a change in Irish law to a primogeniture method of inheritance. Younger sons and any unmarried daughters would have to emigrate in order to make a life for themselves. In fact, the Irish immigrants were unique in the fact that unlike most other European immigrants groups, who generally traveled in the aura of supportive families, most Irish immigrated to America alone, including female Irish immigrants.

The earliest Irish immigrants to Chicago worked on the Illinois & Michigan Canal in the 1830s and 1840s. Irish immigrants also found work in the lumber, railroad, steel and stockyard industries.

Because the vast majority of these immigrants were Catholic, they immediately made inroads into Church leadership positions. Interestingly, despite the fact that other Catholic immigrant groups, such as the Poles, always outnumbered them, the Irish have been dominant in Catholic Church hierarchy for the Archdiocese of Chicago for over 150 years. Since 1843, nine bishops or archbishops of Irish ancestry have led the Chicago Archdiocese. The first Irish bishop, William Quarter, in an effort to address the various needs of the multi-ethnic Catholic diocese, began the uniquely Chicagoan tradition of founding parishes based upon ethnicity instead of upon strict geographical lines, so that each group could practice their faith in accordance with their heritage.

Within the structure of the Chicago Archdiocese, many Irish American women also made an incalculable contribution to the City of Chicago in that female members of Irish religious orders, particularly the Irish-based Sisters of Mercy, taught thousands in Chicago's Catholic parish schools. Two such schools, Holy Family and St. Vincent de Paul, created the foundation for Loyola University and DePaul University. Irish sisters also founded universities such as Barat College, Mundelein College, Rosary College and the University of St. Mary of the Lake, the latter Chicago's first university. They also taught in Catholic high schools and financed the creation of elite academies such as St. Xavier. In addition, Irish religious women opened Chicago's first hospital and first orphanage, along with staffing many other Chicago hospitals and nursing schools.

For the Irish community as a whole, the Catholic parish became the center of the community. Because the Irish arrived speaking the English language, they did not need to create self-contained enclaves like other immigrant groups. Instead, Irish parishes, staffed by Irish religious, supported the Chicago Irish community on its road to economic advancement. Unlike many other immigrant communities that remained in their original, usually industrial settlement areas, the Irish continued to move outward as the city

Irish American Officer Joseph Conant, one of Chicago's Finest in 1946.

President of Ireland, Éamon de Valera, visits with Maureen O'Looney and her daughter, Theresa, in 1969.

and lines of transport expanded. Indeed, by the 1880s, there already existed a strong Irish middle class presence in the outer, newer parts of the city.

The Irish made their way up the economic ladder in a variety of ways. Some used their industrial beginnings as a springboard to trade union leadership, as shown by the fact that Irish Chicagoans led the fight for workers' rights in a number of industries. They were often supported by pro-labor Irish Catholic priests who began neighborhood-level labor movements that would eventually provide an excellent grass roots model for the national leaders of the American labor movement, such as Saul Alinsky and Joseph Meegan.

As was the case in other cities, the Irish Catholics also dominated city firefighter and police departments, city school systems and government offices. Moreover, having knowledge of the English language and the British system of government upon which the American government is based helped the Irish enormously in the area of politics. Although always outnumbered by several other ethnic groups, the Irish successfully created a powerful, multi-ethnic political coalition within Chicago's Democratic party, which has allowed the group to dominate the governance of the City of Chicago for over 100 years; 12 of Chicago's mayors have been of Irish ancestry.

Today Irish American Chicagoans still hold prominent positions in not only Chicago politics, but also in its media, law firms, financial houses, universities, churches, schools, fire and police departments, unions and government offices.

Irish Chicago has become a world-renowned center for Irish culture, not only because it is the home of several St. Patrick's Day Parades and the green Chicago River, but also because it is home to the American Conference of Irish Studies, where serious academic study of Irish history and culture continues to this day.

Chicago has given birth to some of the world's most dynamic and original Irish artists, such as Celtic fiddler Liz Carroll, artistic director Mark Howard, founder of the Trinity Irish Dancers, and dancer Michael Flatley, creator of Riverdance and Lord of the Dance.

Over 160 years ago, Irish immigrants escaped the famine and came to Chicago with the desperate hope for something better. Chicago gave them that opportunity, and they and their succeeding generations have used it well.

Irish American officers march in turn-of-the-century Chicago in front of their "paddy wagon," a derisive name rooted in the anti-Irish stereotype common to that era.

Tom Carroll

Chicago History Museum

A Chicago native and two-time All-Ireland fiddler and composer Liz Carroll poses with fellow performer, John Doyle.

Proud Irish American police officers at a Chicago St. Patrick's Day Parade.

The Irish American Heritage Center, on Chicago's northwest side, fosters the practice, study and celebration of Irish, Celtic and Irish American cultural traditions. The IAHC houses a 650-seat theatre, an authentic Irish pub, a social center, an excellent library, a museum, dance/music studios and meeting rooms. Below is a bake sale at the IAHC.

Peig Reid/Irish American Heritage Center

Cliff Carlson/Irish American News

Cliff Carlson/Irish American News

Cliff Carlson/Irish American News

Chicago History Museum

Middle: The Irish American Heritage Center, "the house that food built," was a school building remodelled by volunteers from the community who were only compensated through meals.

Above: A beautiful carriage is a fitting vehicle for the St. Patrick's Day Parade Queen.

Left: Irish bag pipers in the 1957 St. Patrick's Day Parade at 79th and Ashland.

CHIEF O'NEILL'S SALMON DISH

INGREDIENTS

4 10-oz. fresh salmon filets

POTATO BOXTY

2 large baking potatoes, peeled and shredded

1 garlic clove, minced

1 small red onion, diced

1 bunch green onions, chopped

1 egg

½ cup cooked bacon (about 6 strips), chopped

½ cup all-purpose flour

LEMON CAPER SAUCE

1 shallot, minced

4 tbsp. butter

1 lemon, juiced

½ cup white wine

4 tbsp. capers

1 cup heavy cream

Salt and pepper to taste

Salmon: Salt and pepper fish filets and roast in a pre-heated 350F oven for 10 minutes.

Potato Boxty: Sauté garlic, red and green onion, and bacon for about 3-4 minutes on high heat, then cool slightly. Add flour, potatoes and egg then completely blend all ingredients and form into eight 3" diameter pancakes. Fry on medium heat for 3-4 minutes a side until golden brown and slightly crispy.

Lemon Caper Sauce: Sauté shallots until translucent, add wine and reduce to almost dry. Add heavy whipping cream then reduce by ½ to ¾ volume. Add lemon juice, capers and butter. Season with salt and pepper to taste.

To Plate: Place boxty pancakes in center of plate. Top with salmon filet and pour over both with lemon caper sauce. A mixed vegetable medley or roasted asparagus would be a great accompaniment. Garnish with parsley and a lemon wheel.

SERVES 4

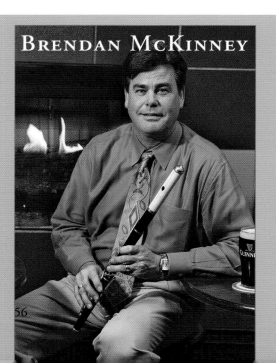

BRENDAN McKINNEY

When the Spanish Armada wrecked off the Irish coast in 1588, an Irish legend says that the ships were carrying potatoes. Some of them washed ashore and the local people gathered and planted them. The history of the Irish is divided into three major periods: before, during and after the potato. When the crops failed, life was devastating for the Irish folk.

Fish, too, was significant, from both the sea and the many inland rivers and lakes. Shellfish was considered the food of the poor, especially mussels that could be gathered without the need for boats. Around County Kerry, where my mother was born, there is an abundance of wild salmon in the rivers and so there are many traditional ways to prepare salmon; but this dish represents one of our family favorites.

My wife, Siobhan, was also born in County Kerry and we both love Irish music and culture. At age 16, I won the title of All-Ireland Bag Piping Champion. I play the uilleann pipes, wooden flute and the penny whistle and my wife is an award-winning wooden flute player.

Being first-generation Irish American (my father was born in County Derry, Ireland), I appreciate how Chicago has welcomed generations of ethnic groups from all over the world. They, in turn, have made great contributions to the community at large. Although I can't live in two places at once, I'm proud to call Chicago my home!

Chief O'Neills

MAUREEN O'LOONEY

On the corner of Belmont and Laramie is a signpost which reads, "Honorary Maureen O'Looney Avenue." It's certainly been a long road from Bohola, where I was born, in the center of County Mayo. Little did I know that the girl who graduated from a convent school and helped her mother in our family store would one day, in the 1950s, visit her aunt in Chicago where she would become, some fifty years later, a well-known resident of the greatest city in the United States. In addition, I was honored to be an hour-long guest on the Oprah Winfrey Show, *played "Governor For a Day" under George Ryan, had dinner at the White House and am a founding member of the Irish American Heritage Center. But my greatest joy is being a "home away from home" for Irish immigrants whom I help find jobs and a place to live.*

After working for United Airlines, I opened an Irish store which recently celebrated its 40th anniversary. Surrounded by imported Irish china, bacon, sausage, sweaters, dancing shoes, Irish newspapers and music, I feel as if I am still in Ireland. Every day fellow countrymen come through the door to share their lives with me. Chicago also has incredible Irish restaurants, pubs and a mayor with Irish roots.

Attached is a hundred-year-old recipe. After the five-year Potato Famine which began in 1845, many Irish reared their own pigs back home and grew vegetables to ensure they would never go hungry again.

TRADITIONAL IRISH BREAKFAST

INGREDIENTS

Kerrygold butter

Irish sausages

Black and white pudding

Tomatoes

Irish bacon

Beans

Pre-boiled potatoes

Pinch of parsley

Brown bread

Typically for an Irish Breakfast, serve each person two slices of Irish bacon, two Irish sausages, two slices of each pudding, two quartered tomatoes and a portion of beans, home fries and eggs.

Place a knob of Kerrygold butter in a frying pan or skillet.

Fry the sausages until golden brown all around. When done, place on plates in warming section of oven.

Slice pudding about ½-inch thick and place in pan with quartered tomatoes. Add in slices of Irish bacon. Over medium heat, fry bacon, puddings and tomatoes until browned on all sides.

Heat beans over medium heat. Stir until steaming hot.

To make home fries, melt a tablespoon of butter in a hot pan. Add pre-boiled potatoes. Fry until golden brown. Plate. Garnish with parsley leaves over tomato.

This breakfast is a full meal accompanied with slices of brown bread and Kerrygold Irish butter. Hot Irish tea is a must. Tea is best made in a teapot where second cups can easily be accessed during the course of the breakfast.

SERVES: THE ENTIRE TABLE

JERRY WINSTON

BOILING BACON

INGREDIENTS

Boiling bacon, either pork shoulder or the
    loin (approx. 3-4 lb. piece)
Large head of cabbage, quartered
2 Spanish onions, diced
4 carrots, thickly sliced
14 red potatoes, cut in half

PARSLEY SAUCE
3 tbsp. butter
2 tbsp. flour

1 cup milk
1 tbsp. white wine
1 cup minced parsley

OPTIONAL
½ cup heavy cream
Parmesan cheese
Horseradish
Garlic

Place boiling bacon in a large stock pot. Fill container with cold water. Be sure to fully submerge the boiling bacon, allowing extra room for the vegetables later. Allow the water to rapidly boil then reduce heat to a simmer. Simmer 30-40 minutes per pound. Forty minutes before the bacon is cooked, add the cabbage, carrots, potatoes and onions. Using a fork, pierce the boiling bacon, to confirm the meat is tender. Remove all items from stock pot. Allow for meat to rest and cool slightly. Drain vegetables in a colander. Slice bacon in quarter-inch slices. Place them on a bed of cabbage with vegetables and potatoes.

Parsley Sauce: Mix butter, flour, milk and whisk while simmering. Add white wine, parsley (or optional seasonings). Continue whisking until desired thickness. Pour over plated boiling bacon.

SERVES 6

Traditions are powerful expressions of family and heritage. Throughout the world, St. Patrick's Day is the hallmark of Irish culture. Such traditions transcend into Irish food and can be experienced in Ireland or in the heart of Chicago.

Benefiting from my Irish roots, I helped introduce boiling bacon to Chicago residents. In Ireland, its popularity stems from the many farms and abundance of pigs in the country. The preparation time to make boiling bacon is minimal which is equally responsible for its popularity. The Irish favor boiling a lot of their food which gets them quicker to the heart of the matter—enjoying it around the dinner table.

As for my boiling bacon recipe, it has been passed down through generations of my family. My father, Michael, a butcher by trade, came to the United States from County Roscommon, and in 1960, with my mother, Mary, founded Winston's Market. In the end all nine of his siblings came to the United States, each pursuing the American Dream.

Our family business has survived on manufacturing, preparing and selling Irish foods, along with the popularity of our market, deli and restaurant. Our specialty for the past 35 years has been boiling bacon, but we also offer favorites like Irish bacon, black and white pudding, corned beef and smoked butt. We hope to continue to thrive in America's third largest city while giving Chicago a fine taste of Ireland.

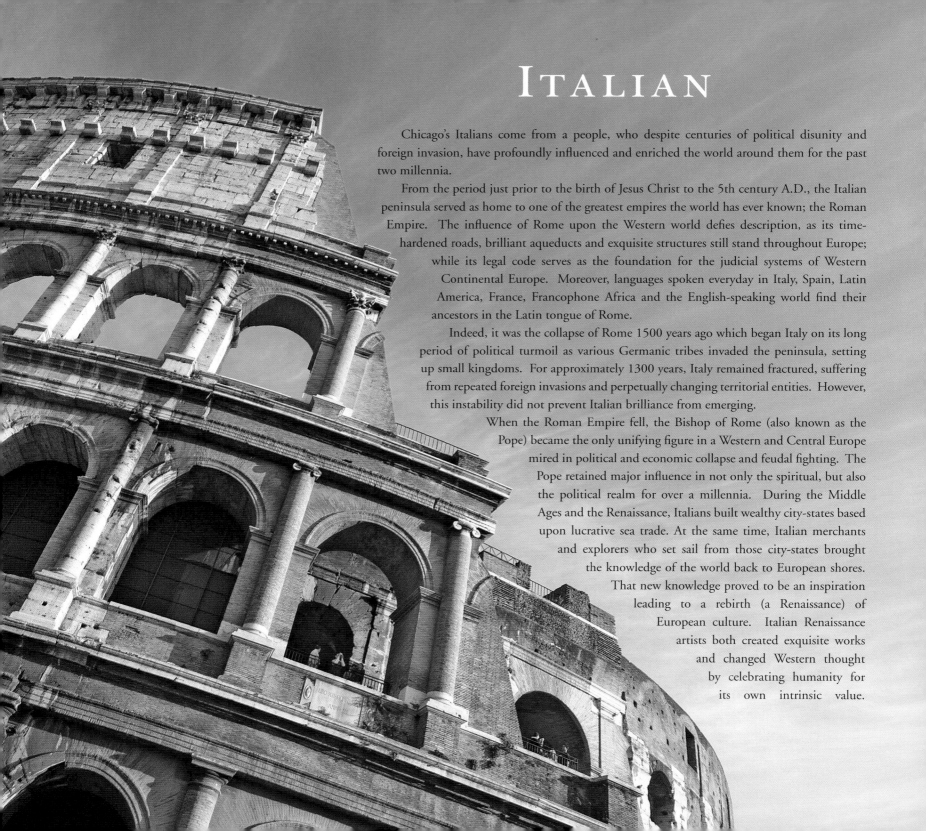

ITALIAN

Chicago's Italians come from a people, who despite centuries of political disunity and foreign invasion, have profoundly influenced and enriched the world around them for the past two millennia.

From the period just prior to the birth of Jesus Christ to the 5th century A.D., the Italian peninsula served as home to one of the greatest empires the world has ever known; the Roman Empire. The influence of Rome upon the Western world defies description, as its time-hardened roads, brilliant aqueducts and exquisite structures still stand throughout Europe; while its legal code serves as the foundation for the judicial systems of Western Continental Europe. Moreover, languages spoken everyday in Italy, Spain, Latin America, France, Francophone Africa and the English-speaking world find their ancestors in the Latin tongue of Rome.

Indeed, it was the collapse of Rome 1500 years ago which began Italy on its long period of political turmoil as various Germanic tribes invaded the peninsula, setting up small kingdoms. For approximately 1300 years, Italy remained fractured, suffering from repeated foreign invasions and perpetually changing territorial entities. However, this instability did not prevent Italian brilliance from emerging.

When the Roman Empire fell, the Bishop of Rome (also known as the Pope) became the only unifying figure in a Western and Central Europe mired in political and economic collapse and feudal fighting. The Pope retained major influence in not only the spiritual, but also the political realm for over a millennia. During the Middle Ages and the Renaissance, Italians built wealthy city-states based upon lucrative sea trade. At the same time, Italian merchants and explorers who set sail from those city-states brought the knowledge of the world back to European shores. That new knowledge proved to be an inspiration leading to a rebirth (a Renaissance) of European culture. Italian Renaissance artists both created exquisite works and changed Western thought by celebrating humanity for its own intrinsic value.

Following the Renaissance, Italy entered a period of foreign domination during which various European states, including France and Austria, ruled parts of the Italian peninsula. This time of foreign domination came to a close after Italian nationalists succeeded in their decades-long fight for full Italian unity and independence, known as the Risorgimento in 1870.

Chicago's Italian community began slowly, starting with a modest number of arrivals in the 1850s. For the next 30 years, Italian immigration continued at a slow pace, with only 1,357 Italians living in the city as late as 1880. They made their living in middle class occupations, such as barbers, artisans, vendors and restaurateurs. Some even became wealthy with wise investments in real estate.

This early group hailed mainly from the Italian province of Liguria. Several of these early immigrants had participated in the Risorgimento. Thus, as a group, early Chicago Italians were very passionate in their Italian patriotism. They introduced this zeal to Chicago, from which Italian-nationalist mutual benefit societies and newspapers were born, in addition to the founding, in 1868, of Chicago's first Columbus Day Parade.

But with the turn of the 19th century, Italian immigration increased dramatically. However, these new immigrants were not financially comfortable Risorgimento veterans who had time to celebrate and discuss the glories of the Italian State. Instead, they were peasants escaping the poverty of small farms and an almost feudalistic land economy in the southern Italian-speaking regions of Basilicata, Campania and the oft-invaded Mediterranean island of Sicily.

Advertisements showing a demand for laborers on America's rapidly expanding railroad lines, for which Chicago served as a major hub, brought Italian peasants to the city. Once in Chicago, exploitative labor bosses, known as *padrones*, organized them into work gangs. The laborers would then be sent to various sites around the country, wherever a new railroad line needed to be built.

As was the case with many other groups, the southern Italian men arrived first. Once they settled into a stable job, they sent word home of their success, causing not only wives and children, but also brothers, cousins and fellow villagers to follow. As such, Chicago Italians followed a pattern of chain migration, with later-arriving men working in factories, the railroad or public works departments. With regard to the women, they often worked in the garment industry, doing piecework at home or in dark and dingy sweatshops, or they took in boarders.

The culture of the southern Italians was one of loyalty to fellow townsmen, or *paisani*. Attachments between the *paisani* manifested itself in a variety of ways. In urban tenements, fellow *paisani* lived together in the same buildings in an attempt to replicate the village community. Southern Italians formed mutual aid societies comprised of *paisani* from the same Italian villages. The society was often named for the patron saint of their village.

Regrettably, this intense loyalty to region and village allowed factionalism to grow within the Italian community, sometimes rooted in centuries-old interregional antipathies, but just as often based upon some recent conflict. Middle-class Italians, such as professionals, *padrones* and merchants, tried to achieve unity among Italians through nationalistic pride. But, the organs of these unifying

Chicago History Museum

Dominic Candeloro

A turn-of-the-century Italian immigrant couple.

Jane Addams' Hull House, at Polk and Halsted, was a place where Italian immigrants were welcome.

efforts, including newspapers such as *L'Italia,* merely promoted the positions of already well-situated Italian Americans. As such, they could not bring unity to a community that, as of 1912, had approximately 400 *paisani*-based organizations.

Though overwhelmingly and often devoutly Roman Catholic, the institutional Church did not unify the Italian as it did the Chicago Irish. Due to various historical factors, in particular, the Vatican's stance against the unification of Italy, many Italians viewed priests with an anti-clerical eye. Italians often expressed their Catholicism through village-based traditions kept alive by Italian women, and by the veneration of patron saints. However, over time, and with the assistance of priests who could respect their point of view, the Italian community eventually became much more involved with the Catholic parish scene.

Unfortunately, this long-term disunity made Chicago Italians more vulnerable to vicious anti-Italian stereotypes and prejudices that even respected newspapers perpetuated during the late 19th and early 20th centuries. Indeed, though the vast majority of Italians never engaged in illegitimate activities, they suffered discrimination in employment and housing.

World War I provided a catalyst that relieved some of the effects of that discrimination, if not the prejudice itself. First, Congress enacted legislation restricting immigration in response to the war, thereby cutting off the seemingly never-ending supply of immigrant labor. This lack of new workers combined with the American mobilization for war led to labor shortages, which caused industry owners to accept Italian workers when they previously had not.

Though still predominantly working class, Italians prospered in trucking, factory and construction work prior to the Great Depression,

Italian Chicagoans in Depression-era housing at Sibley and Taylor Streets.

Left: The Napoli Store at 28th and Drake in 1914.

Background: The home of an Italian immigrant family in 1898 in Chicago's Little Hell neighborhood.

increasing their upward mobility. The Italians in the garment and construction industries also became instrumental in the founding of labor unions.

The turmoil of the 1930s brought the Great Depression and Chicago Italians suffered like the rest of America. During this period, they overwhelmingly favored the New Deal politics of President Franklin Delano Roosevelt and they became solid fixtures in the city's Democratic base. The 1930s also saw an increasingly powerful Benito Mussolini. Strong national pride persuaded many Italian Americans to support the fascist dictator, but that all changed when Pearl Harbor was bombed in

1941. Japan, Germany and Italy had been allied as the three major Axis powers, so America quickly joined the worldwide fight against their tyrannical dictators. Thousands of Chicago Italians joined the Armed Forces and worked in the defense industry to support the American war effort.

Following the war, the G.I. Bill allowed great numbers to attend university and to buy homes. The benefits of the G.I. Bill helped Italian American Chicagoans to begin their meteoric rise, which is evident among the 500,000 Italian Americans who call Chicago home today.

Above: A stunning float at 2007's Columbus Day Parade.

Right: Early students at Assumption School.

Far right, top to bottom:
- *Young Italian Americans at 2007's Columbus Day Parade.*
- *A classic Italian barber.*
- *Federal agents confiscating distillery equipment. Sadly, the actions of a few in the Prohibition Era caused law-abiding Italian Chicagoans, which constituted the vast majority of the community, to often be unfairly stereotyped.*
- *First Holy Communion in 1966 at St. Anthony's Church.*
- *Christopher Columbus and Queen Isabella at 2007's Columbus Day Parade.*

65

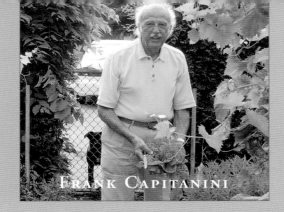

FRANK CAPITANINI

We have a garden that my father, Alfredo, planted in 1925, a year after we came to America and just before he opened the Italian Village Restaurant in 1927. To this day, we still import our seeds from Italy and grow most of the tomatoes, lettuce, vegetables and spices used in our recipes. It's a tradition that gave my father great pleasure and gives our whole restaurant family pride.

My father always took a family approach to our business. Situated in the Chicago Loop, the area, over the last 80 years, has seen many economic changes. (Our menu once read: Spaghetti and Meatballs: 40 cents.) However, many of our employees have worked for us for over 40 years, some over 50. Today, Alfredo and Gina Capitanini are third-generation owner-operators of this world-famous restaurant.

The original recipe for Chicken Alfredo was brought to Chicago by my father. We served the dish here first, at our own restaurant. Many have tried, but failed, to impersonate it. Other versions will mistakingly include peas. With its rich undertones of garlic, oil and spices, it is a perfect example of Northern Italian cuisine.

Many of the recipes, such as the Chicken Alfredo, are over a hundred years old. Being the oldest Italian restaurant in Chicago, we have seen the world change but one thing remains the same: the familial warmth of our hospitality and the generous patronage of the people of Chicago.

CHICKEN ALFREDO ALLA VILLAGE

INGREDIENTS:

1 whole 3-lb. chicken, cut in 12 pieces
6 garlic cloves, peeled
⅛ tsp. each dry rosemary, salt, pepper
4 large mushroom caps

4 mild Italian sausage links
1 cup olive oil
½ cup white wine
6 small potatoes, peeled

Preheat oven to 450F.

Rinse chicken and pat dry with paper towel. In a large heavy-bottomed skillet, heat olive oil to 350F. Carefully add potatoes and cook until light brown on all sides. Remove potatoes to drain on paper towel. Drain off all but ¼ cup of oil and return skillet to stove. Carefully add chicken (skin side down) cooking four minutes until brown then turn to brown other side for four minutes. Remove to plate. Add sausage pieces to brown on all sides.

Return chicken to skillet. Add garlic cloves, seasonings, mushrooms and browned potatoes. Toss gently to coat and distribute seasonings. Place in preheated oven and bake for 20-25 minutes until cooked to 175F.

Remove skillet from oven, then carefully drain oil from skillet. Over medium heat, add white wine and simmer for 2-3 minutes. Remove chicken to serving platter, arrange potatoes and sausage then pour pan juices over all.

SERVES 4-6

Grandfather Alfredo Capitanini, founder of Italian Village.

Interior of Italian Village.

**PEGGY GLOWACKI &
ROSE LODOLCE GLOWACKI**

When I was growing up, my family would alternate—and sometimes combine—the Polish and Sicilian foods of our heritage.

The recipe of these fabulous cookies came from my Sicilian grandmother, an immigrant from Altavilla Milicia, a small town outside Palermo. Each generation has changed and adapted the recipe.

Eating was never perfunctory in our house. Meals were talked about, anticipated and savored. The foods we shared were an integral part of my childhood.

In a third-generation household of two nationalities, most ethnic customs have been lost over time. Food, however, was one of the main links to our melded Polish and Sicilian heritage. We made the effort to bring our world together around a dinner table. It was great fun, and it made for wonderful memories.

At Easter, my mother (photo above, at right) would always make prodigious quantities of her Easter Basket cookies; so much that it was a pleasure to share with all of our neighbors.

PUPA CU L'OVA
(ITALIAN EASTER BASKET COOKIES)

INGREDIENTS

1 dozen hard-cooked eggs in their shells

4 cups flour plus ½-1 cup flour

1 cup sugar

1 tbsp. baking powder

1 tbsp. corn starch

1 cup melted but slightly cooled vegetable shortening

2 oz. melted but slightly cooled butter or margarine

3 eggs

1 tbsp. vanilla

½ cup milk

Sift all dry ingredients into a large bowl. Make a well in the center and add the slightly cooled, melted vegetable shortening and butter, three eggs, vanilla and milk. Mix with a spoon to moisten and then knead in the bowl with your hands, adding one-half to one cup additional flour if necessary to make dough stiff enough to handle. Divide dough into thirteen portions. Roll and flatten dough into 12 three-inch wide circles. Make decorative cuts at an angle around each circle's edges and place on baking sheet. Lightly press one dry, hard-boiled egg into the center of each cookie. Roll last dough portion into a thin handle to drape across the egg. Secure ends by pressing into the dough. The recipe should make approximately twelve baskets. Bake in a 350 degree oven for twenty minutes or until lightly golden. Let cool. Frost with a confectioner's sugar frosting and decorate with candy sprinkles.

MAKES 12

The foods we eat have a history and what we put on the dinner table is shaped by geography, economics, religion and tradition. Although some foods may change over time, their meanings and memories endure. As an historian and archivist, I am interested in what food says about who we are and who others think we are.

Dominic Candeloro

An old-fashioned gelato ice stand.

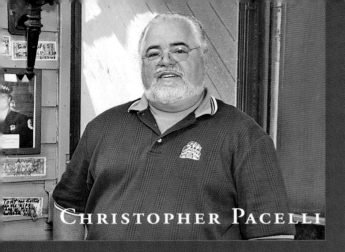

CHRISTOPHER PACELLI

Four generations ago, my grandparents developed the term, "Italian Beef" when they began selling sandwiches to doctors at the Rush University Medical Center on Polk Street. Because the meat was very expensive, my grandparents sliced the beef extra thin and added Italian spices.

Today, this sandwich, known as Al's Italian Beef, has been perfected in Chicago. The family business began at a little curbside stand in 1938 at the corner of Laflin and Harrison streets. Because of the sandwich's popularity, the business moved to its present location at 1079 West Taylor Street in the heart of Little Italy.

Joining my grandfather was my uncle, Al Ferreri, and my parents, Frances and Chris Pacelli, Sr. The latter added a type of "au jus" or beef gravy to the sandwich. The beef is free of preservatives; only fresh ingredients are used because it makes for the best and healthiest sandwich of its kind. And now, nearly 70 years after our little curbside stand was established, the business continues to be successful throughout Chicagoland.

Included, at right, is a family favorite recipe, inherited from Grandma Baptista, a meatball and gravy dinner. Consistent with Italian tradition, the term gravy aligns itself with a marinara sauce. The flavor of this gravy is enriched by its pork-based ingredients.

MEATBALLS & GRAVY

INGREDIENTS

GRAVY

3 cans tomato purée; plus 3 cans water
6 oz. finely grated Pecorino/Romano cheese
3 bay leaves
¼ cup garlic powder
⅛ cup garlic salt
⅛ cup oregano
⅛ cup parsley flakes
1 slab meaty baby back ribs, cut up
½ tsp. minced garlic
Extra virgin olive oil
8 fresh basil leaves

MEATBALLS

3 lbs. ground beef
1 lb. ground pork (or veal)
1 medium onion, finely
   diced
1½ cups bread crumbs
⅛ cup parsley
⅛ cup oregano
4 oz. Pecorino/Romano
   cheese, finely grated
   (plus more for garnish)
3 tbsp. garlic salt
½ tbsp. garlic powder
3 eggs

GRAVY: In a braising pan, pour enough olive oil to just cover the pan's bottom. Place minced garlic in pan, heat for several minutes (do not burn garlic) then remove garlic. Brown baby back ribs in pan; when done, place aside. In a large stockpot, empty three cans of tomato purée. Place an equal amount of water (three cans) into the stockpot. Add ribs and remaining ingredients. Stir. Leave on low to medium heat so as to braise the ribs. While simmering, you have time to prepare the meatballs.

MEATBALLS: In a large bowl, mix together ground meats. Create a well in the ground meats center; add all remaining ingredients to center of well. With both hands, combine the entire mixture together. Take mixture and make into 2" or 2½" meatballs. Place in pan and cook meatballs in a 350F oven. Turn the meatballs over once and continue to cook. Place meatballs and ribs in the stockpot with the gravy to simmer.

Simmer gravy 2 to 2½ hours and stir often. When the gravy is complete, remove the meatballs and ribs and place in a separate bowl on table.

Choose your favorite pasta, cook it to *al dente* (according to the package instructions). Place about two ladles of gravy into the bottom of a serving dish. After draining the pasta, immediately add to serving dish. You should have enough gravy so the pasta doesn't stick together. In a separate serving bowl, provide additional gravy with ladle so as to allow your guests to add more or less gravy.

Garnish with additional Pecorino/Romano cheese according to taste. Serve with a hearty and crusty Italian bread and a great glass of wine!

SERVES 6-8

TURANO FAMILY

Our grandfather, Mariano Turano, was a talented baker. He came from Castrolibero, a small "paese" (village) in the province of Calabria in Southern Italy. This area was renowned for wheat farmers and bakers of artisan breads in the village's stone oven. In 1958, my grandfather moved his family to Chicago hoping that America would provide greater opportunities.

In 1962, he founded the Turano Baking Company on the west side of Chicago. He and his sons produced and delivered their hearth-baked breads to homes in the neighborhood. As his reputation grew, the local grocery stores began selling his breads.

Today, Turano Baking Company is still family-owned and operated. From old-world French and Italian bread to "ciabatta" (Italian for "slipper" because of its flat shape), European sandwich rolls to biscotti and assorted "dolci" (confections), we continue to bake using time-tested techniques, not just from Italy but from all over the world.

Turano's popularity originated in Chicago with a pizza recipe passed on from our Southern Italian ancestors. A delicious family favorite, Mamma Susi Pizza is named for its creator, our grandmother Assunta. It is a traditional Calabrese focaccia, a flavorful dough topped with "pomodori" (tomatoes) and various cheeses reminiscent of the homemade pizza "Nonna" (grandma) used to bake almost daily.

72

MAMMA SUSI PIZZA

INGREDIENTS

DOUGH

2 cups warm water (about 105 degrees)

2½ tbsp. extra virgin olive oil + 2 tbsp. for greasing pan

½ oz. dry yeast

1¾ lbs. all-purpose flour (extra for rolling out dough)

¾ oz. salt

Cornmeal (or flour) for dusting pan

PIZZA

9-10 Roma plum tomatoes, sliced

1 cup fresh basil leaves, thinly sliced

1 lb. fresh Mozzarella, thinly sliced

2 tbsp. olive oil

Kosher salt

. . . .

In a 4- or 5-quart bowl, combine water, olive oil and yeast. Allow to ferment for five minutes. Add yeast water to the flour and salt, then mix on medium speed for about five minutes or until the dough is elastic. If dough is too wet, you may add flour a little at a time until moist but not too sticky. Remove from mixer and cover tightly. Place in a warm spot and allow to double in size (in about 30 minutes). Pre-heat oven to 350 degrees.

Brush a 11¾"x 16½" sheet pan with oil; dust with cornmeal. Roll out dough on floured surface to ½-inch thick, transfer to sheet pan, allow to raise for another 15 minutes then dot surface with a fork. Bake in center of oven for about 8 minutes or until slightly browned. Remove from oven. Arrange sliced tomatoes (covering entire surface) and add slices of fresh Mozzarella, layered slightly under tomato slices.

Return pizza to oven, continue to bake until cheese melts and begins to brown around the edges. Remove from oven, allowing to cool slightly, then sprinkle with basil leaves and Kosher salt to taste.

Buon Appetito!

SERVES 4-6

A Jewish presence existed in Chicago from virtually the very birth of the city in the 1830s. However, unlike most of the other ethnic groups which have made Chicago their home, the Jewish immigrants did not leave a precious homeland from which their families and the people of their nationality possessed roots dating back millennia. For the Jews were already in a state of exile when they boarded ships for America.

Expelled from their Middle Eastern homeland by the Roman Empire around 70 A.D., the Jews found homes of exile in the Roman territories encircling the Mediterranean, the Middle East and Western Europe. As a minority population wherever they settled, they lived an often dangerous, always precarious existence. Due to religious, and later, racial discrimination in Europe, Jews could not own land in many European kingdoms, were forced by royal edict to live in "ghettos" that were locked from the outside with the coming of nightfall, and as a vulnerable minority, were often viciously and violently blamed for misfortunes that might befall a region, such as murders, plagues or droughts. Such horrific group scapegoating led to the expulsion of Jews from major nation-states such as England and France for several centuries, and to many regional massacres of Jews during the time of the Black Death. Thus, by the 19th century, the bulk of European Jewry lived in Central and Eastern Europe.

The first significant group of Jewish immigrants arrived in Chicago in 1841, from mostly German-speaking territories. Most arrivals enjoyed spectacular economic success, starting as modest street peddlers and ending up as business magnates, founding companies such as Florsheim,

A stained glass window from an early synagogue on display at Chicago's Navy Pier.

JEWISH

Inland Steel and Hart, Schaffner & Marx. Indeed, as early as the Great Chicago Fire of 1871, many members of this initial group could afford to live in affluent lakefront communities.

These early Jewish immigrants also founded Chicago's first synagogue, Kehilath Anshe Mayriv, in 1847. Moreover, this small enclave displayed superb organizational abilities and strong community loyalty, as shown by the fact that as early as the late 1850s, as many as 15 thriving Jewish organizations existed in Chicago. In fact, in 1859, these groups united under the umbrella of the United Hebrew Relief Association.

However, it was not until the late 1870s that large-scale Jewish immigration to Chicago began. Though all found their religious roots in Judaism,

these latter immigrants differed greatly from the middle class German Jews who had arrived in Chicago a generation earlier.

Firstly, the late 19th-century Jewish immigrants generally did not come from Germany, as their earlier brethren, but rather, they came from Eastern European countries such as Russia and Poland. Here autocratic rule was common, where nobles and oligarchs controlled much of the wealth, and where Jews faced institutionalized oppression, locked ghettos, and in certain areas, violent pogroms. Many of the Eastern European Jews who disembarked at Chicago left behind a life of brutal rural poverty.

Yet, this combination of oppression and deprivation caused the Eastern European Jews to not only hold tight to their fellow Jews, but also to their faith. Thus, these often formerly ghettoized newcomers practiced a much more Orthodox form of Judaism and kept closer to the Jewish community than the more Reform-minded, assimilated Jews of the 1840s. In fact, the Eastern European Jewish immigrants were so committed to living with fellow Jews that they actually created a neighborhood on Maxwell Street that was not unlike a rural Jewish village, called a *shtetl*, which one might have found in Eastern Europe during that era. Maxwell Street was home to not only countless small peddlers and artisans selling their wares, but also Jewish family residences, Jewish social service institutions, Hebrew schools and approximately 40 synagogues.

From their starting point on Maxwell Street, the Eastern European Jews also worked in factories, particularly in the garment industry, where a number of Jews would discover and crystallize their allegiance to workers' rights and would eventually

Always an immigrant gateway, starting in the 1880s, Maxwell Street welcomed Eastern European Jews who created a vibrant neighborhood, not unlike a rural Jewish village or "shtetl" in Eastern Europe, full of thriving street markets, Hebrew schools and over 40 synagogues.

Chicago History Museum

play a strong leadership role in the American labor movement.

Other Eastern European Jewish families achieved great economic success by creating, developing and expanding small businesses, often with the assistance of family and neighbors.

Further, German and Eastern European Jewish families alike held education in high regard, and it was not uncommon for poor Jewish parents to work terribly hard so as to allow their children to remain in school. This dedication to education combined with community support for Jewish-owned businesses permitted many Jews by the 1920s to move beyond Maxwell Street and into more affluent neighborhoods, including German Jewish neighborhoods.

By the 1930s, Chicago had the third largest urban Jewish population on Earth, behind only New York and Warsaw. They numbered 270,000, approximately 9% of the entire population of Chicago. And though some cultural barriers had existed between the German Jews and the Eastern European Jews (the latter making up 80% of the total Chicago Jewish population), the Jewish community began to unify within institutions founded in the late 19th century by German Jews to help their Eastern European brethren in their transition from "European" to "American." Later, the two sides of the community became further unified by their mutual commitment to education and by their community-wide economic success. Finally, any residual divisions disappeared with the end of World War II, as all Chicago Jews stood together not only horrified at the atrocities committed by the Nazis and the unfathomable tragedy of the Holocaust, but also with pride in their faith, heritage and Middle Eastern homeland of Israel.

In the post-war era Chicago Jews achieved even greater economic successes as the benefits of the G.I. Bill helped many Jewish veterans to purchase single-family homes, and as the decline of anti-Semitic restrictive covenants allowed Jews to move into affluent suburban enclaves for the first time.

Today, approximately 189,000 of Chicagoland's 270,000 Jews live in the suburbs, particularly in those north of Chicago. Moreover, though Chicago's Jewish community no longer has a central, Maxwell Street-like neighborhood, the needs of the community are most definitely addressed as hundreds of well-organized, Jewish-centered religious, cultural, social, political, charitable and educational institutions can be found throughout the Chicagoland area, each contributing not only to the Jewish community, but also to the betterment of Chicago.

Indeed, the impressive success of the Jewish community of Chicago is testimony to the power of the human spirit. The Jews who immigrated to Chicago found in their roots the profound sadness of exile and the potentially scarring memory of oppression. Yet, after enduring a few decades of imperfect freedom in Chicago, they showed the world that when hard work is combined with a loyalty to community and tradition, along with a respect for education, those labors can bear amazing fruits.

Chicago History Museum

A Maxwell Street shopkeeper in the 1950s.

Chicago History Museum

A bustling market scene on Maxwell Street in 1917.

Marshall Rosenthal

Samuel Beckett

KAM (Kehilath Anshe Maarav) Isaiah Israel Temple, established in 1847 in Hyde Park, claims to be the first synagogue in the Midwest.

In 2007, a Jewish Chicagoan stands by the shore of Lake Michigan at Evanston on Yom Kippur to contemplate Judaism's most solemn holiday.

LAURA FRANKEL

As a professional kosher chef for the past 10 years and a kosher "mom," I am always looking for unique global foods to use in my cooking—both personally and professionally.

My style of kosher cooking is to take what is naturally kosher—unprocessed and whole ingredient foods—and turn them into wholesome and innovative kosher dinners. I have discovered many options, but my favorites come from the Mediterranean, in particular Moroccan lamb. This dish is a lamb tagine which combines the natural flavor of the meat with rich aromatic spices and selected fruits.

After the Jewish expulsion from Spain and Portugal, the Jews carried with them their Mediterranean recipes. Like all of us, Jewish people, wherever they go, share culinary preferences with neighbors and friends. I am no different.

My Jewish heritage and love for kosher food has helped establish my career as the executive chef for Wolfgang Puck Catering at the Spertus Institute for Jewish Studies. This experience led me to write Jewish Cooking for All Seasons Cookbook.

In Chicago, a lively city like no other, people are willing to try new food styles. It is this receptivity that makes kosher cooking enjoyable and fun.

LAMB TAGINE

INGREDIENTS

LAMB

3 lbs. lamb shoulder, cut into 2-inch cubes

6 medium carrots, peeled, thickly sliced

2 large Spanish onions, peeled and diced

2 fennel bulbs (white part only), diced, reserve fronds for garnish

8 large garlic cloves, chopped

½ cup pitted dates, cut in half

½ cup dried figs, cut in half

½ cup dried apricots, cut in half

2 heaping tbsp. tomato paste

2 tbsp. charnushka

3-4 cups chicken stock

CHARNUSHKA
MOROCCAN SPICE MIX

2 2-inch cinnamon sticks

1 tbsp. whole coriander seeds

1 tsp. cumin seeds

1 tsp. crushed red chiles

½ tsp. fenugreek

½ tsp. anise seeds

1 cardamon pod

1 tbsp. dark brown sugar (optional)

GARNISH

Preserved lemons

Cilantro, chopped

Harissa hot sauce

Lamb: Preheat oven to 325F. Place lamb chunks on a sheet pan or cutting board. Pat dry meat to ensure browning. Season lamb with salt and pepper. Brown lamb in batches in a large sauté pan coated with olive oil over medium heat. Be sure to scrape up any browned bits left behind. Remove browned lamb to a Dutch oven (also called a tagine). Brown vegetables in batches in the same pan. Remove vegetables to the Dutch oven. Lightly sauté garlic until it is fragrant; about one minute. Be sure not to brown the garlic.

Place remaining ingredients in the Dutch oven. Cover and cook for two hours until the lamb is tender and sauce has thickened. Garnish with preserved lemons, chopped cilantro and at the table pass round the harissa. Lamb tagine can be made and stored covered in the refrigerator for up to two days before serving. It can also be frozen for up to one month.

Charnushka Moroccan Spice Mix: Place all ingredients in a spice grinder or coffee grinder and process until completely ground. Store covered at room temperature for up to six weeks.

SERVES 6

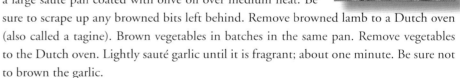

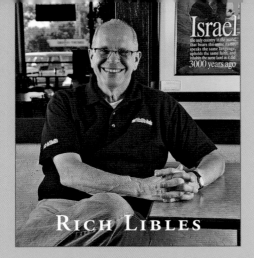

RICH LIBLES

Our Da'Nali's Café was founded in 1996 in Skokie in Chicago's flower capital—on every corner there is a "Rosenblum." As for me, I was raised in Hyde Park but my father was born in Warsaw and made his way to Des Moines where he met my mother.

People often ask me, "Why Italian food kosher-style?" and I remind them that, outside of Israel, Italy houses the world's oldest Jewish community. We cater predominantly to religious Jews and so everything is made with Kosher cheese, milk and flour under the supervision of the Chicago Rabbinical Council.

Customers order fries with their pizza. Our fries, coated with flour and salted, are the world's finest. They can be ordered spicy, with cheese or garlic.

I picked up this eggplant parmesan recipe from Piccolo Angelo's in the West Village in New York City. Most eggplant parmesan are too burnt, watery and "overcheesed." Using small amounts of tomato, basil and cheese, we make a delicate, lighter dish.

Our restaurant is family-friendly. The children love the painted blue skyline on the ceiling and are encouraged on special nights to make their own pizzas and sushi. Some of Chicago's best photographic talent adorn our walls. Saturday night is Club Da'Nali with live music an hour after Shabbat.

EGGPLANT PARMESAN

INGREDIENTS

3 lbs. eggplant (2-3)

2½ lbs. ripe plum tomatoes (quartered) -or-1 can
    (28 oz.) plum tomatoes in purée (roughly chopped)

¼ tsp. salt, or to taste

Freshly milled white or black pepper

1 cup all-purpose flour for dredging

Safflower oil for frying

Unsalted butter for greasing the baking dish

Lightly toasted, fine, dried bread crumbs

¼ cup fresh basil, chopped

1 lb. fresh mozzarella, thinly sliced or shredded

½ cup freshly grated Parmigiano cheese

. . . .

Eggplant: Cut stems and navels off eggplants then cut crosswise into rounds ¼-inch thick. Sprinkle each slice lightly with salt. Place the rounds in a colander, standing them upright for 40 minutes.

Tomato Sauce: Cook tomatoes uncovered over gentle heat, stirring until thickened, about 40 minutes. Remove from heat and let cool slightly, then pass tomatoes through food mill. If sauce is too thick, return to saucepan and simmer gently up to 20 minutes longer. Season with salt and pepper. Pour flour on a sheet of wax paper. Season with salt and pepper. Use paper towel to blot salt and sweat from eggplant.

In a skillet over medium-high heat, pour oil to a depth of one inch. Heat oil until hot enough to make eggplant sizzle. Once oil is hot, but not before, dredge several eggplant slices in flour, shake off excess and slip into oil. Fry on both sides, eight minutes total. Drain well on paper towels. Similarly, fry remaining slices.

Preheat oven to 400 degrees. Butter a 10"x 14" baking dish and coat with the crumbs, shaking out any excess.

Blot each slice of eggplant before placing a layer in the dish. Add a little of the sauce, some chopped basil, then a layer of mozzarella and finally a sprinkling of Parmigiano. Continue layering the ingredients in this order, ending with a layer of eggplant smeared with sauce and sprinkled with Parmigiano and remaining basil. Bake at 400°F for 20 minutes.

SERVES 4-6

A.L.T., a dream combination of avocado, lettuce and tomato, is a Kosher attempt to replicate the B.L.T.

A performance of traditional Lebanese dance in Chicago in 2006.

Sam Daou

LEBANESE

The first Lebanese immigrants began entering Chicago in the 1880s. The group would steadily migrate to the Windy City until the launch of World War I in 1914.

Though the present-day descendants of those immigrants would identify themselves as Lebanese based upon the geographical region from which their ancestors originated, the arrivals carried with them documentation which indicated a homeland within the Ottoman Empire, or more specifically "Ottoman Syria." At the turn of the 19th and 20th centuries, the region known in English as Ottoman Syria, in Arabic as *bilad al-Sham*, consisted of a large area encompassing not only present-day Syria, but also present-day Lebanon, Jordan, Palestine and Israel.

Lebanon was the beautiful northwest of this region, with its entire western side bordering the Mediterranean. In this region roughly equal Muslim and Christian populations lived together, with a vast majority of the Christians following the Lebanese Maronite tradition. The Maronites are a part of the Roman Catholic Church; however, they are considered Eastern Rite Catholics in that they practice their Catholicism within the context of Eastern Orthodox traditions.

The Lebanese immigrants who arrived in Chicago during the turn of the 19th and 20th centuries were almost exclusively Christian. Though most left Ottoman Syria for reasons of overpopulation and declining economic conditions, the Lebanese immigrants did come from a variety of occupational backgrounds, as some had been born into the Lebanese peasantry, while others entered Chicago as talented artisans or savvy entrepreneurs. In fact, a particularly astute group of Lebanese peddlers introduced Chicagoans to the gorgeous wares of the Middle East when they set up shop at Chicago's World Columbian Exposition of 1893. Street peddling would become a popular occupational choice for these immigrants, as would dry-goods retail and the textile trade.

The Lebanese built a neighborhood with their fellow Syrians centered between California and Kedzie avenues and 12th and 15th streets. Just prior to the beginning of World War I, this community numbered approximately 3,000 strong. But with the coming of the war, Lebanese immigration all but stopped as Congress enacted laws restricting immigration, including that from regions such as the Ottoman Empire, which upon entering the war, the United States would call enemy.

The defeat of the German-Austrian-Ottoman coalition would ring the death knell for the

Ottoman Empire. Two of the victors, France and Great Britain, would divide Ottoman Syria amongst themselves, thereby creating not only modern-day Syria, Jordan and Palestine, but also laying the foundation for the political strife that continues to plague the region today.

However, in Chicago, the Lebanese community prospered, founding Lebanese-centered organizations and clubs, and their own Maronite Church, Our Lady of Lebanon, in 1948. In fact, one of the nation's most famous Lebanese Americans, Muzyad Yakhood, more popularly known as Danny Thomas, belonged to this parish. Mr. Thomas had a strong devotion to St. Jude, which was fostered by the Claretian Missionaries and their National Shrine of St. Jude on Chicago's South Side. He turned to the Chicago Lebanese when he was trying to raise funds for the building of St. Jude's Hospital in Memphis, Tennessee. St. Jude's is now one of the top childhood cancer research centers in America, thanks in no small part to donations received from Chicago's Lebanese community.

During the mid-20th century, Chicago's increasingly Americanized Lebanese community steadily continued its rise up the economic ladder, and until the turbulence of the late 1960s and early '70s, it appeared as if the Lebanese immigration story was reaching its conclusion. But with the beginning of the sectarian-based Lebanese Civil War in 1975, it became readily apparent that another chapter yet needed to be written.

The devastating civil war and the political factionalism and terrorism that followed left Lebanon in a ruinous state until at least the late 1990s. To escape the turmoil, both Muslim and Christian Lebanese from professional and entrepreneurial backgrounds immigrated in large numbers to several American cities, including Chicago. The arrival of these Lebanese immigrants has proven to be an absolute gift to the City of Chicago, as virtually from the moment they arrived, the professional Lebanese began contributing to the community as doctors, attorneys, engineers and pharmacists. Moreover, the entrepreneurs among them opened shops, bakeries, grocery stores and restaurants, thereby providing jobs and stabilizing neighborhoods. Most importantly, these immigrants have infused not only the Chicago Lebanese community with a new vigor, but also the larger Arab community, thus making Chicago one of the most vibrant Arab American centers in the United States.

The World Columbian Exposition was held in Chicago in 1893. The Lebanese community made its first major mark on the Chicago community at this Exposition, as Lebanese traders found great success in selling wares of the Holy Land at this venue.

Chicago History Museum

MAUREEN ABOOD

Middle Eastern culture is a rich facet of Chicago's ethnic diversity. Sitting at a Lebanese table, you discover a deep link between our food and our sense of self. I am a second-generation Christian Lebanese American. During culinary demonstrations, I share about my family and how the Lebanese are known for their warm hospitality and good food. Unfortunately, because we are the crossroads of the Middle East, we have known war, division and unrest.

My grandmother, Sitto, kept three staples in her refrigerator in Lansing, Michigan: black olives, "kimaj" (pita bread) and "labneh" (a tart, creamy spread made from homemade yogurt; Arabic for "white").

Every meal is accentuated with "hummus" (Arabic for "chickpea") and labneh yogurt spread (in photo at right, directly below flowers) which are both eaten with Lebanese bread. In the Lebanese kitchen they are also excellent as "mezze" (appetizers) and served as accompaniment to most main dishes – even breakfast!

By sharing these foods and my family stories, I hope I am extending the beautiful warmth and love that my parents and grandparents passed on to me. By doing a few small things, we can truly open the hearts of others.

TOASTED PINE NUT HUMMUS

INGREDIENTS

1 15-oz. can chickpeas, drained and rinsed thoroughly

½ cup toasted pine nuts, plus 1 tbsp. for garnish

1 tsp. salt

1 garlic clove

¼ cup tahini (sesame paste)

¼ cup lemon juice, freshly squeezed

2 tbsp. water

2-3 tbsp. extra virgin olive oil, plus more for garnish

1 tbsp. parsley, chopped

In blender or food processor, pulse to combine chickpeas, pine nuts, salt, garlic, water and tahini. Stop occasionally to stir.

Add olive oil and lemon juice, stopping occasionally to scrape down the sides. Blend until very smooth.

Spread hummus on a small plate. Drizzle with olive oil and sprinkle with toasted pine nuts and parsley. Serve with fresh pita bread.

SERVES 6

LITHUANIAN

The story of the Lithuanians in Chicago is a tale of a nation dead to all the world, except to those who knew it best, its sons and daughters. It is the story of those knowing children who over time traveled across the ocean to a city built on prairie land, where through more than a century of love, faith and work, they helped nurse their nation back to life.

The Lithuanian people find their roots in an Eastern European tribe first mentioned in written history in the first decade of the 11th century. By the 13th century, the Lithuanians had united under their first Christian king, Mindaugas, who was crowned King of Lithuania by the Pope himself. Mindaugas would be the only king of the Baltic nation, as later rulers would take the name of Grand Duke.

By the end of the 14th century, the Lithuanian Grand Dukes succeeded in achieving a fortuitous alliance with Poland, and by 1410, this Lithuanian-Polish alliance defeated their main rival, the Germanic Teutonic Order, thereby securing territories in present-day

Belorussia, Russia and Ukraine. At the zenith of its power, the Polish-Lithuanian Commonwealth stretched from the Baltic Sea in the north to the Black Sea in the south.

But by the second half of the 18th century, a weak central government and repeated battles with their Austrian, Prussian, Russian and Swedish neighbors had taken such a toll on the Lithuanian-Polish alliance that by 1795, most of the Lithuanian Grand Duchy fell under Russian control. Subsequent uprisings brought down the wrath of Czarist Russia: including the suppression of the Catholic religion in favor of the state-sponsored Russian Orthodox religion and the first deportations of Lithuanian dissidents to Siberia.

Therefore, when Lithuanian immigrants began to come to Chicago in large numbers at the turn of the 20th century, their documentation read Imperial Russia, as there was officially no such nation-state as Lithuania.

Yet, love for the old country still burned bright. This love was exemplified by the fact that, even though most of the early Lithuanian immigrants came to Chicago illiterate, a blatant indicator of the poverty and oppression that had been inflicted on their homeland, the vast majority had no intention of staying in America. Rather, they wished to earn money in economically booming Chicago, and then return home with full pockets, thereby allowing for a better life in Lithuania. But, of course, as was the case with many immigrant groups who planned for short stays, the great possibilities for prosperity and community in America eventually persuaded them to stay and send for brides and families. Indeed, many of those who did return to Lithuania came back to Chicago, as they could no longer tolerate the oppressive, rural poverty.

However, the first several years in America proved difficult. Most of the early immigrants were young, single men. Arriving in "The Hog Butcher of the World," many found work at the Union Stockyards in Bridgeport, on Chicago's South Side. In fact, Lithuanian residents of Back of the Yards were made famous by Upton Sinclair's 1906 novel, *The Jungle*, as the wretched conditions these immigrants endured in the stockyards served as the real-life basis for the literary work.

Yet, through all the struggle, by 1914, Chicago was home to the largest urban Lithuanian population on Earth. From this population sprang schools and churches, including St. George's Church in Bridgeport. They established their own building and loan association in Bridgeport in 1897 (born in the backroom of a neighborhood saloon), and two more by the end of World War I. In addition, two Lithuanian banks opened around the turn of the century, followed by an insurance company and a Lithuanian newspaper, *Lietuva* (Lithuania). In 1919, the *Draugas* (Friend) daily newspaper organized and continues to serve the Lithuanian community.

World War I soon brought German troops to Lithuania. This German occupation awakened a fervor for independence among the Lithuanians, which grew as Germany's military situation weakened. In 1917, Lithuanian politicians assembled in Vilnius, and a year later, boldly declared the independent state of Lithuania, even while the German army still controlled most of the country.

As a result, native Lithuanians became less attracted to the prospect of overseas immigration. Moreover, in the 1920s, the U.S. government instituted new restrictive immigration policies. Thus, the number of new Lithuanians arriving into Chicago dropped sharply.

In the following years, Chicago's Lithuanians became increasingly involved in their American home, including participation in Chicago politics on both the Republican and Democratic tickets.

But Chicago's Lithuanian community had not forgotten their native homeland, as shown by the introduction of basketball to Lithuania by Chicago Lithuanians in the 1930s. The homeland took to the game immediately, and to this day, basketball remains their number-one sport.

Lithuania's brief taste of independence was tragically short-lived, as Adolf Hitler and Joseph Stalin's infamous secret political pact led to Lithuania succumbing to Soviet occupation by the fall of 1939. Interestingly, the Soviets found themselves in Lithuania after the defiant Baltic State refused to side with Germany and invade neighboring Poland.

Soviet occupation, however, again ended with the German Army's successful invasion of Lithuania in June of 1941 and the expulsion of Soviet troops.

In the summer of 1944, the Soviet Army once again crossed the borders of Lithuania, and sadly, in accordance with the Yalta and Potsdam agreements between the Soviet Union, the United States of

Vienybė (Unity) initially founded in 1886 by J. Paukszys in Plymouth, Pennsylvania.

Balzekas Museum of Lithuanian Culture

Chicago History Museum

Chicago History Museum

"Hog Butcher to the World!" Lithuanians found work at the Union Stockyards in Bridgeport on Chicago's south side; their struggles were made famous in Upton Sinclair's 1906 novel, The Jungle.

87

America and Great Britain, the Baltic States were absorbed into the U.S.S.R.

The end of World War II brought great change to Chicago's Lithuanian community. After Stalin's Red Army occupied Lithuania, sponsored refugees of Lithuanian descent flooded into America, especially Chicago. The city's Lithuanian community fervently opposed the Soviet occupation via organizations such as the Chicago-based American Lithuanian Council, the Supreme Committee for the Liberation of Lithuania, and the World Lithuanian Community.

The new post-war émigrés reinvigorated the Chicago community and the number of Lithuanian-based organizations proliferated.

Nevertheless, Chicago's Lithuanian culture began to take divergent paths during the years of Communist control in the homeland. Major émigré groups, which were often Chicago-based and Catholic-centered, believed that connection to Lithuania should be made solely on a private basis,

so as to never give an ounce of recognition to the Communist government they firmly opposed.

Other émigrés, organized in a group known as *Santara-Sviesa*, took a different approach. They encouraged more relations with Lithuania, in order to expose the people there to international thought and to create a unified Lithuanian culture. The group became famous for smuggling books into Communist Lithuania in the 1970s and '80s.

With the crumbling and eventual fall of the Soviet Union, Chicago Lithuanians continued to work tirelessly for the independence of their homeland, by lobbying Congress and sending money to political groups in Lithuania. These efforts helped unite Lithuanians on both sides of the ocean to a degree that had not been seen for at least a century. Thus, when Lithuania became an independent state in 1991, many daring young Chicagoans returned to their native land, some to a land they had never seen, demonstrating idealism to the concept of a free Lithuania. In recognition

for their efforts, Chicago declared the Lithuanian capital city of Vilnius as a "sister city" in 1992.

Then in 1998, a century after the beginning of Lithuanian immigration to the United States, the Chicago-Lithuanian connection came full circle when Valdas Adamkus, a Chicagoland Lithuanian, left the comfort of his suburban Hinsdale neighborhood, returned to a free Lithuania and was elected president of the Lithuanian Republic.

Ursula Astras, director of folk art workshops at Balzekas Museum of Lithuanian Culture, organizes Easter egg decoration classes.

Balzekas Museum of Lithuanian Culture

A well-attended Lithuanian American banquet. From 1914 to 1939, there were more Lithuanians in Chicago than in Lithuania's capital of Vilnius.

Balzekas Museum of Lithuanian Culture

Part of the 1921 graduating class of Holy Cross School in Marquette Park.

Balzekas Museum of Lithuanian Culture

88

A Marquette Park statue, erected in 1935, honoring Lithuanian American aviators, Steponas Darius and Stasys Girenas, shown at right. Darius and Girenas were known for their historic crossing of the Atlantic on July 15, 1933, in 37 hours, without landing.

The life-long dream of Stanley Balzekas, Jr., to preserve for posterity the wealth of material pertaining to Lithuania's history and culture was realized when he opened the Balzekas Museum of Lithuanian Culture on Archer Avenue in 1966. The museum moved to this spacious location on Pulaski Road in 1986.

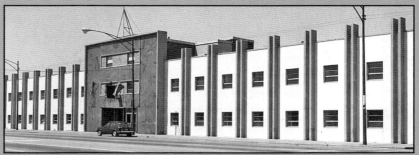

A 2005 performance of Cavalerica Rusticana by the Lithuanian Opera Company. The group celebrated their 50th anniversary in 2006.

The Tenth Annual Lithuanian Song and Dance Festival. Held at the Rosemont Horizon, in Rosemont, Illinois (shown at left and above). More than 40 dance groups, comprising more than 2000 dancers, aged 7 to 70, perform simultaneously, their dancing creating a kaleidoscope effect of moving patterns.

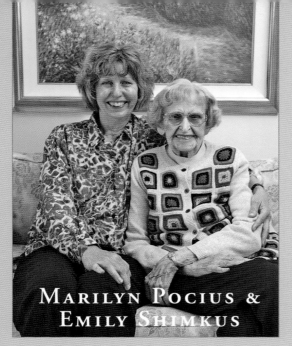

**MARILYN POCIUS &
EMILY SHIMKUS**

*I love to explore the markets of Chicago and appreciate the diversity
of the city's cuisine and, through this, my own diverse background. My
cookbook,* A Cook's Guide to Chicago, *is a foray into the wonderful
ethnic stores in the greater Chicago area.*

*My father's parents came separately from Lithuania and met and
married here in the United States. My mother's relatives
came over from the Isle of Man with Roger Williams, one
of the founders of Providence, Rhode Island. My mother's
background was very American. I consider myself a
"mutt," which is very American, too.*

*This recipe for gruzdis comes from my father's sister,
Aunt Emily (photo above, at right). Considered a treat,
it is nothing more than fried dough and very much
like the Polish dessert "crullers," also called "bow ties."
Gruzdis hold a special place in my heart as I remember
my grandmother making them for us when I was a child.
She packed them in a brown paper sack and dusted them
generously with powdered sugar. When we brought them
home and opened the bag, the powdered sugar would
make everyone sneeze. They seemed exotic to me at the
time, but mostly delicious.*

90

AUNT EMILY'S GRUZDIS

INGREDIENTS

3 egg yolks

3 tbsp. sugar

5 tbsp. sour cream

1 tbsp. rum (or brandy)

¼ tsp. vanilla

¼ tsp. almond extract

¼ tsp. salt

2¼ cups flour, sifted

. . . .

Beat yolks until light. Add sugar gradually and continue
beating. Add sour cream, rum, vanilla, almond extract and salt;
mix well. Add flour a little at a time until a ball of dough forms
(you may not need all of the flour). Knead by machine
or on a floured board until dough is no longer sticky
when cut. Divide dough into two or three balls, wrap
in plastic and let rest at least ten minutes.

Heat oil for deep frying to 375F. Roll out dough
paper thin on floured board (Aunt Emily never did
this, but the easiest way is to run the pieces through
a pasta machine just as you would pasta dough—start
with a setting of One and end with Five). Cut into
3"x 1" strips. Cut a slit in the middle of each strip and
bring one end through the slit. Deep fry a few at a time
for about three minutes on each side. Drain on paper
towels. Sprinkle with powdered sugar before serving.

SERVES 10-12

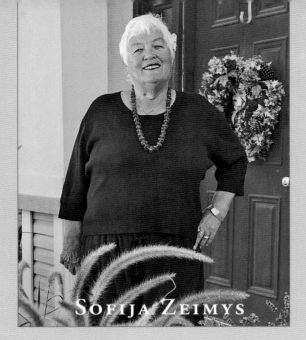

SOFIJA ZEIMYS

The United States Bicentennial will always hold special meaning for me. For it was on this day, July 4, 1976, that I became a U.S. citizen. I came to America in 1950, when I was 24, amidst the World War II aftermath and Soviet occupation of the Baltic States. I spent five years in an allied-run camp for war refugees in Kassel, West Germany before the Displaced Persons Act of 1948 allowed my husband and I to enter America.

A special food that I brought from Lithuania, and learned to cook from my grandmother, is kugelis, a potato pudding that has European similarities, including the Jewish kugel and the potato pancake from Central and Eastern Europe. Kugelis has evolved as a very hearty peasant dish that takes advantage of Lithuania's abundant and perennial crop of potatoes as well as pork.

Interestingly, at least to me, is how many cooks in Lithuania keep their recipe a secret—or, at minimum, they leave out one primary ingredient so they can have their own "best" kugelis recipe.

Even though I am proud to be an American, my family and I still celebrate many Lithuanian customs, as part of the religious celebration of Easter and Christmas. It is mandatory to serve kugelis which helps me celebrate my heritage while embracing my new life in my new country!

92

KUGELIS
(POTATO PUDDING)

INGREDIENTS

5 lbs. Idaho white potatoes	1 cup heated milk
6 eggs, beaten	1 tbsp. sour cream
1 lb. bacon	1 tsp. salt
1 medium onion, finely chopped	1 tsp. white pepper
	1 tsp. ascorbic acid (or 4 vitamin
1 stick butter	C tablets, crushed)

Peel the potatoes into a large bowl (years of experience have proven Idaho potatoes make the best kugelis). Cover with cold water. One by one, remove potatoes from water and finely grate. Add liquid ascorbic acid (or crushed vitamin C tablets) to the accumulating grated potatoes.

Cut bacon into small pieces then add to a 12" or 14" frying pan. Cook on medium heat and stir occasionally. When the bacon is very lightly cooked, add chopped onion. Although it can be a minor balancing act, the bacon should be almost cooked through while the onions are translucent. Remove from heat then add butter to the bacon and onions; stir until the butter's melted.

Into the grated potatoes, pour the bacon and onions. Stir lightly and add the six beaten eggs, salt, pepper and sour cream. Mix thoroughly.

Liberally butter a 9"x 13"x 2" Pyrex-type (which controls excess edge browning) glass pan. Pour in potato mixture.

Bake in 425F preheated oven for 30 minutes. When kugelis shows slight browning around the edges of the pan, bring oven temperature down to 350F and cook another 45-60 minutes until top is golden brown. Cover pan with aluminum foil and cook another 30 minutes until pudding is firm. Slightly shake pan to test. Remove from oven, then let rest 30 minutes.

Serve as a stand alone entrée or as a side dish. Top off with a generous dollop of sour cream. If you double this recipe, it's best to use two 9"x 13"x 2" pans rather than one large one. The cooking will be uneven with a larger pan.

SERVES 10

MEXICAN

During the 19th and early 20th centuries, the nation of Mexico endured a series of never-ending catastrophes, including the loss of one-third of its nation to the United States, radically unstable government, and a violent revolution during the first part of the 20th century. Thus, when recruiters, termed *enganchistas*, brought to Mexico a message of a peaceful Chicago full of more jobs than industry could possibly fill, many Mexicans answered the call.

The first large group of Mexican immigrants arrived in Chicago in the 1910s, with their numbers rising dramatically in the 1920s. This was in large part due to the fact that industrial lobbyists persuaded Congress to not include Mexicans in the Immigration Act of 1924, a statute that successfully restricted the entry of many other countries.

Most of the initial Mexican immigrants were middle-class men, who had been born in the Mexican states of Guanajuato, Jalisco and Michoacán. Sadly, when these Mexicans arrived, they quickly discovered that the *enganchista* had left many important details out of his tempting tales of Chicago. For these Mexicans found that the housing units available were overpopulated, dilapidated and overpriced. Moving into neighborhoods on the Near West Side, in South Chicago, and the Back of the Yards, Mexicans often paid rents much higher than the average immigrant due to anti-Mexican prejudice among many landlords. As a result, Mexicans often had no choice but to share flats with one another, thereby only exacerbating the unhealthy and overcrowded status of these housing units.

Moreover, though Mexicans did find both semiskilled and skilled work in agriculture and the steel, railroad and meatpacking industries, many who arrived with the promise of good work found themselves in the distasteful position of taking the place of striking European workers, thus breeding anti-Mexican feeling among European communities.

As such, Mexicans often lived together in enclaves called *colonias* within larger multi-ethnic neighborhoods. *Colonias* sprang up in the Back of the Yards, Calumet, South Chicago and on the Near West Side. Within the *colonias* one could find restaurants, tortilla factories, *bodegas* (small food shops or delis), Spanish-language newspapers, workers' associations, mutual aid and fraternal organizations (or *mutualistas*) which served the needs of the Mexican community.

In the *colonias*, Mexicans created thriving communities where they primarily practiced Roman Catholicism and successfully founded Mexican-centered parishes including South Chicago's Our Lady of Guadalupe and St. Francis of Assisi on the Near West Side. They also celebrated events like Cinco de Mayo, which commemorates the Battle of Pueblo against the French invasion of Mexico in the mid-19th century; and Mexican Independence Day on September 16th.

Unfortunately, the arrival of the Great Depression dealt a terrible blow to the *colonias*. When local industry began to feel the effects of the spiraling economy, discriminatory practices among management often led to Mexicans being among the first employees dismissed. As such, many Mexicans in Chicago suffered from long periods of unemployment during the 1930s. To make matters worse, the poor economic climate fanned the flames of racism to the terrible extent that local groups, such as the American Legion of East Chicago (with the blessing of the American and Mexican governments), forced hundreds of unemployed people who "looked Mexican" to gather up their families and to get on trains bound south for Mexico. This practice of forced return decimated the Mexican population of Chicago so severely that by 1940 almost half of the people of Mexican descent, including many U.S. citizens, had been deported.

However, the labor shortages that occurred as a result of World War II gave those Mexicans still living in Chicago a newfound power. Industries, desperate for workers, had to accept Mexican employees and furthermore attend to Mexican worker demands, as the latter supported unions in great numbers during this time.

With the end of the war, Mexicans still stood firmly for workers' rights as exemplified by an incident in 1947. During that year, Inland Steel, a company whose workers were on strike, brought 250 Mexicans to Chicago for the purpose of making the Mexicans strikebreakers. This time the Mexicans refused to work, signed up with the union of the striking workers, and walked into the offices of Inland Steel demanding a paid trip home. The 1940s and '50s also witnessed the founding of several Mexican civil rights' organizations which combated anti-Mexican racism.

With the advent of the 1960s, the *colonias* of South Chicago and the Back of the Yards were still going strong, but the *colonia* of the Near West side was destroyed by the construction of the University of Illinois at Chicago. The Mexicans of that neighborhood moved to Pilsen, or *La Diesiocho*, as residents called it after "18th Street," which ran through Pilsen. By the mid-1970s, this *colonia* had grown past 26th Street. This expansion was called Little Village or *La Villita*, or *La Veintiseis* for "26th Street."

Today, both *La Diesiocho* and *La Veintiseis* remain thriving *colonias*, bustling with stores, businesses, restaurants and colorful murals that reflect the Mexican flavor of the area. Moreover, though Mexican community-action groups are still needed to fight against discrimination and to serve the needs of this still rapidly growing immigrant community, with a population numbering more than 1.1 million in the Chicagoland area, the Mexican voice is loud, clear and powerful.

This doll is an artifact commonly found during El Día de los Muertos (Day of the Dead) a celebration honoring past lives of loved ones. The celebration occurs on the 1st and 2nd of November.

95

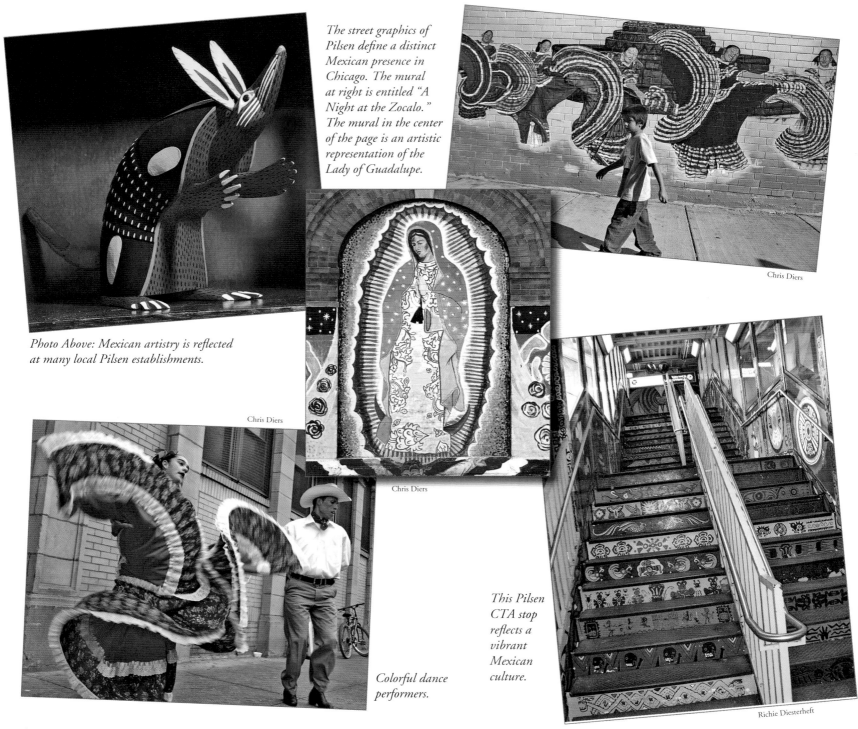

The street graphics of Pilsen define a distinct Mexican presence in Chicago. The mural at right is entitled "A Night at the Zocalo." The mural in the center of the page is an artistic representation of the Lady of Guadalupe.

Chris Diers

Photo Above: Mexican artistry is reflected at many local Pilsen establishments.

Chris Diers

Chris Diers

Colorful dance performers.

This Pilsen CTA stop reflects a vibrant Mexican culture.

Richie Diesterheft

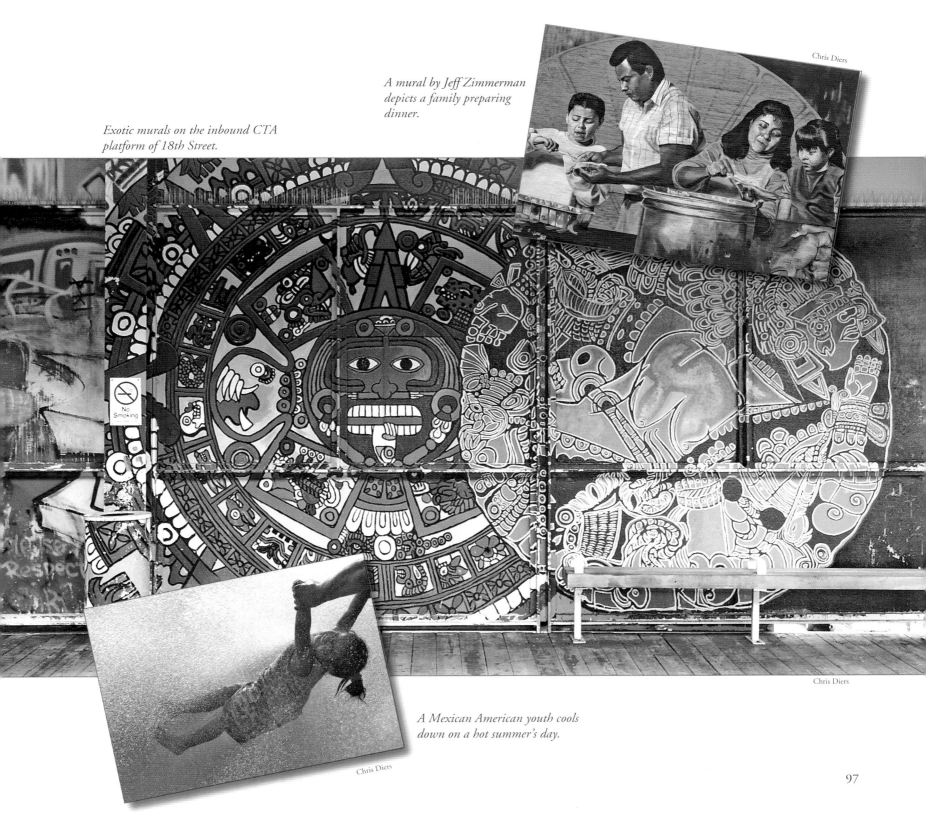

Exotic murals on the inbound CTA platform of 18th Street.

A mural by Jeff Zimmerman depicts a family preparing dinner.

Chris Diers

A Mexican American youth cools down on a hot summer's day.

Chris Diers

97

TERESA FRAGA

I came to the United States as a little girl, crossing the Rio Grande River into Texas and struggling with the tremendous adjustment of leaving behind friends and entering a new way of life. I spoke Spanish but, in my new American school, that was cause for discipline. My life experiences in the United States have shaped who I am today. I remember speaking "Spanglish" words or switching fluidly from English to Spanish in mid-sentence. Over the past forty-one years, I have come to enjoy living in my new hometown—Chicago.

My upbringing in Mexico and Texas has influenced my eating and cooking habits. For me, enchiladas are a staple menu item for my family and many Mexican Americans. Originating in Mexico, enchiladas are filled with carrots, potatoes, grated cheese, onions and either chicken or beef. Typically, the sauce which covers enchiladas is "mole poblano" (a blend of dried chile peppers, ground nuts, spices and Mexican chocolate), as opposed to Texas where the filling is grated American cheese with onions then topped with chili con carne (at right).

Although not a chef by trade, I have one dish, my specialty, which I feel can compete with almost any chef—my enchiladas potosinas, a festival dish usually prepared outdoors.

Living in Pilsen, a Mexican community in Chicago, has given my family a sense of stability and a firmer economic foothold. I am thrilled to have learned to cook many traditional Mexican dishes and to make a contribution to my community so that all of us in Pilsen will be proud to call this Chicago community our home.

98

TEX MEX ENCHILADAS

INGREDIENTS

1 dozen corn tortillas

2 cups grated American cheese

1 cup diced onions

½ cup oil

3 cups chili con carne

. . . .

Heat oil in a skillet. Dip tortillas briefly into hot oil (to soften the tortilla). Place on a paper-towel-lined platter (to drain excess oil) and repeat until all tortillas have been preheated.

Heat the chili con carne in a saucepan. Pour a thin layer of the chili into a baking dish, enough to cover bottom of dish (this makes for a softer enchilada). Lightly spread cheese and onions onto a tortilla, roll tortilla and line enchiladas in baking dish side by side. Once all the tortillas are arranged, pour remaining chili on top of the enchiladas. Sprinkle any remaining cheese and diced onion on top.

Bake in a 350F oven for about fifteen minutes -or- microwave on high for 3-5 minutes, until cheese is completely melted. The dish can be served with rice, beans or a fresh salad.

SERVES 6-8

BRYAN GARCIA

As a cook who hails from Mexico City, I take great honor in sharing my recipe of "brochettes al pastor" (shepherd's kebabs) in this book and in our Agave Restaurant. This entrée is popular in Mexico, although it has been adapted from the Middle Eastern spit-roasted meat sandwich known as "shawarma." The sandwich was introduced to residents in Mexico City and in Puebla as these places are home to a large Lebanese population. Mexicans quickly modified the sandwich to our tastes by substituting marinated lamb or chicken with thinly sliced pork, serving them on corn tortillas (instead of pita bread) and adding a pineapple topping.

I learned of this dish from my father who was a taco connoisseur. He always knew where to get the best ingredients for tacos. He was particularly fond of a little taqueria near Chapultepec Park whose name I can't recall since we always referred to it as "Los Tacos al Pastor." Every time we went to the park, we would cap the day's events with a visit to that shop. It was fascinating to see the "pastorero" (taco maker), using his saber-like knife to shave the roasted meat onto the tortilla, fling a slice of pineapple through the air and catch it in the taco in his other hand.

After I came to the United States, I began searching for the best tacos al pastor, only to be disappointed every time. I decided to try and replicate the dish using standard kitchen equipment. My mother sent me her original recipe, which I then modified until I found the perfect balance of international flavors.

100

BROCHETTES AL PASTOR

INGREDIENTS

*3 lbs. pork tenderloin, cut in
    one-inch cubes*

*1 large ripe pineapple, peeled, cored
    and cut in one-inch cubes*

*2 red onions, layers separated and
    cut in one-inch squares*

12 ancho peppers, seeded

5 garlic cloves

½ cup oil

*¼ cup Spanish pimenton (smoked
    paprika)*

1½ cups pineapple juice

1 tsp. oregano

Pinch of cumin

Salt to taste

Over medium-low heat, fry peppers in oil one by one for a few seconds on each side. Soak in hot water for ten minutes. Meanwhile, fry garlic in the same pan until golden brown. Set aside and reserve the oil. Drain peppers and discard soaking water. Place the peppers, garlic, pineapple juice, pimenton and spices in a blender then blend until very smooth. Strain through a fine sieve. Cook sauce in the reserved oil then lower heat to simmer for ten minutes. Check for seasoning and let cool.

Assemble brochettes alternating onion, pork and pineapple slices. Using a brush, apply sauce liberally. Marinate for at least three hours or overnight. Cook for 10-12 minutes over medium heat grill at 400F or hot oven at 500F (or until internal temperature is 165F).

Serve with warm corn tortillas, freshly chopped cilantro and onions, salsa and lime wedges.

SERVES 6

DUDLEY NIETO

Although my mother is from Mexico and my father from Spain, I have lived in Chicago for 28 years. Yet, my feet and soul are planted in all three places. This recipe, like myself, is a subtle blend of influences.

As a young boy, I had a passion to cook. At every opportunity, I cooked for my Boy Scout troop and intently watched my grandmothers preparing flavorful food. But truly it was my father, a fantastic chef, who inspired my passion.

Not only is this pork tenderloin upscale because of the Native Mexican and Spanish "adobo" (red chile sauce) influence, it also has a touch of Arabic. Additionally, combining the chiles, herbs and spices with tequila or vinegar, a Spanish influence, adds a sense of smokiness. This recipe comes from my grandmother who was born in Puebla, Mexico.

The two rich cultures of my parentage give me a sense of security. Looking at the next generation of Mexicans, I see how they are an essential part of the City of Chicago and its progress. This city embraces my dreams and helps me reach the high standards necessary to live a good life.

Currently, I serve as executive chef of Zocalo Restaurant and Tequila Bar, bringing the tastes of the Yucatan, Oaxaca and even the beaches of Acapulco to the Chicago doorstep.

LOMITO AL PASTOR
(PORK TENDERLOIN ADOBO)

6 7-oz. pork tenderloins
MARINADE
*8 oz. guajillo chile, lightly
    toasted, seeded and deveined*
*8 oz. ancho chile, lightly toasted,
    seeded and deveined*
3 cups hot water
1½ Spanish onions
16 oz. apple cider vinegar
½ oz. ground black pepper
1 oz. ground white pepper
1 oz. thyme, fresh
1 oz. oregano, fresh
1 oz. marjoram, fresh
½ tbsp. cumin, ground
2 garlic cloves
½ piece Mexican cinnamon
1 oz. allspice
18 oz. pineapple juice

CREAMY TOMATILLO SALSA
½ cup vegetable oil
5 tomatillos, cleaned
2 jalapeno chiles
¼ piece Spanish onion
2 garlic cloves
Salt and pepper to taste

PINEAPPLE RELISH
*¾ pineapple, peeled, cored,
    diced small*
1 red onion, diced small
*1 serrano chile, washed and
    diced*
1 bunch cilantro, fresh, chopped finely
2 garlic cloves
Salt and pepper to taste
GARNISH
¼ pineapple, cut in wedges
1 red onion, cut in half

Marinade: Soak ancho and guajillo chiles in warm water until soft. Add the rest of the ingredients. Using a blender grind all ingredients until fine consistency. Strain chile mixture through a medium sieve. Marinate pork tenderloin by rubbing on adobo marinade for better results.

Heat two tablespoons vegetable oil in a sauté pan until hot (but not smoking). Sear all sides of the tenderloin to keep juices inside. Finish in preheated 450F oven until medium level of doneness (150-165F internal temperature).

Creamy Tomatillo Salsa: Heat vegetable oil in a saucepan. Add ingredients and simmer at medium heat for 15 minutes or until tomatillos are soft. Transfer salsa to cold pan and cool for 10 minutes in an ice bath. Blend until fine consistency is reached. Salt and pepper to taste.

Pineapple Relish: Mix ingredients in a stainless steel bowl then salt and pepper to taste.

To garnish, cut remaining pineapple into wedges and grill. Cut onion in half and grill. Cut the tenderloin along the bias and plate it making a half-moon shape of tomatillo salsa on side of plate. Place pork tenderloin along the mirror's way and place the relish on top of the pork slice.

SERVES 6

NATIVE AMERICAN

Thousands of years before the first English- and French-speaking immigrants set foot on the land bordering Lake Michigan, Native Americans lived here. They loved and worked, celebrated and grieved, established trading posts and built tribal nations powerful in strength, community and culture. These nations traded with each other, had disputes, made peace and thrived in the land that was to be named after one of their tribes.

Among the tribal nations that lived in the Chicago region prior to European habitation were the Ojibwe (Chippewa) and the Ojibwe-rooted Potawatomi, Ottawa and Odawa nations. In this region also lived the Ho-Chunk, the Menominee, the Miami, the Oneida and, of course, the Illinois. All of these tribes sustained a strong presence in the Lake Michigan region until the coming of the Europeans en masse starting in the late 18th century.

The Europeans brought a hunger for land as well as deadly bacterial and viral strains which had long-incubated in the inhabitants of Europe, but which had never been encountered by the Native American immune system. As a result, many fell to frontier expansion or disease, sapping the strength of once powerful tribal nations.

Another blow was dealt to the Native peoples of Chicago when they became overwhelmed by the advantage the Europeans had in terms of weaponry. Tribes like the Ojibwe, the Ho-Chunk, the Miami, the Potawatomi and the Illinois were forced to cede their lands in the form of treaties with the young American government. The loss of tribal lands caused many Native people to move west. However, a minority of Native families remained, living among settlers throughout the 19th century.

Yet, by the turn of the 19th century, much of the Native population throughout the U.S. either lived in sparsely populated areas or had been forcibly relocated by dictate of the federal government to reservations.

Native Americans remained there in large part until the federal government instituted a so-called "relocation program," starting in the 1950s. This program, seen as controversial and even destructive by many Native Americans, assisted thousands in their move from reservation to city in the 1950s and '60s. Many of these relocating Native people ended their journey in Chicago.

However, some of the new arrivals found the mid-twentieth century urban culture of Chicago to be foreign and radically different from the nature-focused and tribe-centered life on the reservation. In response, Native peoples formed organizations, including the American Indian Center in 1953, to

Black Hawk, famous Sauk Chief (1767-1837).

Chicago History Museum

An artistic representation of Chicago in 1820, showing the land as the Native Americans knew it, before the coming of the Europeans.

Carlos Peynetsa, Native American Chicagoan and proud member of the Zuni nation.

Chicago History Museum

An old postcard shows Native Americans and European Americans mingling at a Chicago train station in 1870.

Dorene Wiese (back row, second from right), proud member of the Ojibwe nation and President of NAES College, celebrates Native traditions with family and friends.

There are several monuments in Chicago that feature Native American subjects.

Chicago History Museum

especially during the 1960s and '70s, as Native Americans founded organizations which addressed their healthcare, artistic, educational, employment and civil rights concerns. The organizations established during that period include the Native American Educational Services (NAES College), Native American Committee, St. Augustine's Center for American Indians, the Institute for Native American Development and American Indian Health Services.

By the year 2000, almost 40,000 Native Americans lived in Chicago, representing almost 100 tribes. Strong Native communities can be found in Ravenswood, Edgewater, Uptown and Rogers Park although Native Americans can also be found throughout the Chicagoland area. With the immense diversity present in Chicago's Native community, the city has become a great cross-cultural center for Native Americans with various languages and traditions represented, not unlike the crossroads ancient tribes formed at the Lake Michigan trading posts centuries ago.

CARLOS PEYNETSA

I am a Zuni, adopted by my Aunt Dora and Uncle Arthur from Isleta, New Mexico. They both worked in Albuquerque, so I was designated the family cook. My grandmother, Lanyateditsa, showed me how to prepare meals to feed my grandfather who worked in the fields. I gathered recipes from friends and girlfriends living in different reservations. At festivals, family reunions, parties and special occasions, I would experiment, ask questions and watch others cook. Tradition in New Mexico dictates that squash, breads and roasts should be cooked in outdoor ovens.

After high school, I came to Chicago in 1965. Graduating from Greer Technical Institute, I was determined to stay and enjoy the "Cement Prairie" and the best skyline in the United States.

The Southwest is "Chili Country." Every village has a variety of hot and spicy recipes using dried or fresh chile pods. These recipes come mostly from my "Nah Nah" (grandmother).

When I am not cooking, I love to sing and dance at pow-wows and perform with the NAES Blackhawk Dance Troupe as well as drumming for schools, festivals and organizations.

I also teach American Indian arts and crafts. To cook, to dance, to sing and to drum is to let your soul fly free.

ISLETA PUEBLO GREEN CHILI

INGREDIENTS

1 lb. ground beef

2 15-oz. cans chili beans

1 can kidney beans

1 46-oz. can tomato juice

1 can whole stewed tomatoes

1 small bunch fresh cilantro, chopped

1 large onion, chopped

1 large bell pepper (green or red), chopped

1 package Chili-o-mix

2 garlic cloves, chopped

4 Hatch's fresh green chile peppers

Brown ground beef. Add to pan and fry chopped bell pepper, chopped garlic, chopped onion and chopped cilantro. Broil or roast, over fire, green chile peppers; peel off the skins and hand split the peppers. At medium heat, heat tomato juice in a covered small pot. Hand mash stewed tomatoes and juice in a bowl then add to pot. Drain excess fat from ground beef and put beef in pot. Add rinsed kidney and chili beans to pot. Add Chili-o-mix, fried green peppers, garlic, onion and cilantro to pot. Salt and black pepper to taste. Cover pot, lower heat and simmer until done; approximately 30-45 minutes.

SERVES 8-12

DORENE WIESE

RAINBOW'S CORN SOUP

INGREDIENTS

1 lb. ground buffalo meat

2 bone-in pork chops

1 lb. white (or yellow) corn, dried

1 acorn squash, peeled and cut in
    one-inch pieces

Salt and black pepper

2 green onions

1 yellow onion

Soak dried corn overnight. In an 8-quart pot, brown both meats and the onions, then add 5-6 quarts of water to simmer for 15 minutes. Add corn and cut-up squash. Salt and pepper to taste. Bring to a boil, then lower heat to simmer 1-2 hours or more.

SERVES 8-12

Sauk Chief Black Hawk believed that "We must continue throughout our lives to do what we conceive to be good. If we have corn and meat, and know of a family that has none, we divide with them. It has always been our custom to receive all strangers that come to our village or camps, to share with them." These are still good words.

Today at 40,000, Chicago is the eighth largest American Indian community in America, larger than most reservations. It is believed that Chicago is an Algonquin word for "wild onion." Years ago, when the buffalo ran free, rich prairies and forests covered every inch of local ground. The Native people cultivated gardens of corn, beans, squash and wild onions. They hunted and fished in the forests and streams nearby.

Corn, beans and squash are called the "Three Sisters" among the Oneida people because they were always planted together and nourished the soil. My uncle, Leon Mike, taught me how to cook the "We Pum a Kedda Ga's" (Rainbow's) corn soup even though he was blind and in a wheelchair. The White Earth Minnesota Chippewa fry bread (photo opposite page, top right), referred to as "dish rags"

by my mother, Doris, is a perfect accompaniment to Rainbow's corn soup. Forming dough into round shapes and throwing them in a frying pan, they resembled dish rags as they bubbled and rose. Eating them hot from the stove, we laughed at the idea that dish rags could taste so good.

My Indian name is White Wing Woman and I am descended from many tribes but go by the name Ojibwe. My uncle, his son-in-law and I traveled throughout this country, singing and praying and laughing. There was nothing better than a good corn and squash soup with fry bread to warm the spirits. Then we knew we were home.

Ray Hanania

PALESTINIAN

The first Palestinian immigrants began arriving in Chicago in the late 19th century. As was the case with the Lebanese and Syrians who arrived during the same period, American immigration authorities deemed the Palestinians' place of origin to be "Ottoman Syria," a region of the Istanbul-ruled Ottoman Empire. Called *bilad al-Sham* in Arabic, this area included present-day Palestine, Israel, Syria, Lebanon and Jordan.

The first Palestinians came to Chicago as traders. When a group of Palestinians found great success selling Holy Land wares at Chicago's World Columbian Exposition of 1893, word spread back home and it convinced many Palestinians to board ship for America. Palestinians continued to immigrate at a steady pace until World War I when an enactment of a more restrictive federal immigration policy caused emigration from most foreign lands to drop off dramatically.

The Palestinians who were actually able to gain entry often found themselves to be markedly different than many of the other ethnic groups that populated Chicago. First, unlike the vast majority

of immigrants to enter Chicago at that time, the Palestinian immigrants were not predominantly Christian; rather, both Muslims and Christians were counted among their numbers. An interesting historical note is that most of the Palestinians who arrived in Chicago during the late 19th and early 20th centuries originated from the same region despite their religious divide. Most of the Christians found their roots in Ramallah, a town geographically situated just north of Jerusalem, while the majority of the Muslims came from Beitunia, Ramallah's neighboring sister city.

Of the Palestinian Christians who arrived in Chicago, most had a history of practicing their faith within the context of Eastern Orthodox Christianity. Though certainly the home of various religions during the late 19th and early 20th centuries, Chicago had few Orthodox or Christian Arab churches to offer these immigrants. As a result, over time, most Palestinian Christians assimilated into more the traditional Western European denominations such as Roman Catholic, Lutheran or Baptist.

Regarding Palestinian Muslims in this initial immigration wave, their entry into Chicago was more difficult compared to their Christian countrymen as they encountered a Chicago which was overwhelmingly Christian and offered virtually no Islamic houses of worship.

Initially, Palestinian families sent their youngest males to Chicago alone with the purpose of earning good money as peddlers, thereby allowing them to support their wives and families and to save for a comfortable retirement back home. Generally, this practice did not change until the second half of the 20th century. As such, most Palestinians either lived in exclusively male boardinghouses or in a space behind their place of business. Indeed, the corner of 18th Street and Michigan is often described as the "Plymouth Rock" of Arab American settlement in Chicago.

From the beginning, Palestinians tended to be a very entrepreneurial group. The early arrivals soon found commercial opportunities within the rapidly expanding African American community. By the 1960s, Palestinians began replacing Jewish shopkeepers as the dominant business owners in the Black Belt, the center of Chicago's African American community. By the 1970s, Palestinians had achieved such a strong commercial presence that shopkeepers with families were able to move out from behind their stores into neighborhoods just west of the Black Belt. But as earlier Palestinians became financially secure and began to increasingly bring over their wives and families, events in their homeland would change Palestine and Chicago's Palestinian community forever.

In 1967, Israel and a coalition of Arab nations fought the third of many wars. Now known as the Six Day War, it ended with the Israeli army occupying Arab lands, including the territory the United Nations had deemed as Palestine in 1947 and the territories known as the West Bank and the Gaza Strip. The war prompted thousands of Palestinians, men and women, both Muslim and Christian, to emigrate. Since 1967, Palestinian immigration to Chicago has steadily increased.

This second wave of immigrants have differed from their predecessors in that they remained strongly tied to their faith of origin, as demonstrated by this group's establishment of many Christian Arab churches and storefront mosques in the Chicagoland area. However, this wave has also followed in the footsteps of their predecessors in that they have proven themselves to be a tremendously entrepreneurial group. Today, Palestinian business owners can be found not only operating shops within minority communities, but they have also carved out niches in the sale and repair of automobiles and in fast-food restaurants. Moreover, in the four decades since the second wave of Palestinian immigration to Chicago began, they have become increasingly wealthy and upwardly mobile. This allowed them to move into suburbs such as Alsip, Bridgeview, Burbank, Cicero, Hickory Hills, Oak Lawn, Palos Hills and, most recently, further southwest into Orland Park, where this rapidly growing population

celebrated the opening of a mosque in 2006.

Yet, despite the successes they have achieved in Chicago, this group remains acutely focused on the political future of their Palestinian brethren in the Middle East. Indeed, many Palestinians live physically in the United States but mentally back home. This nationalistic fervor does not arise merely for ephemeral reasons of ethnic pride, but in a more practical vein as it is hard to find a Chicago Palestinian family that has not been affected by the Six Day War. Family members had to escape the turmoil caused by the war and subsequent occupation. Others are forced to remain in America permanently due to the fact that Israeli law now denies any Palestinian the right to return to Palestine as a resident if they did not live in the West Bank during 1967. Thus, Chicago Palestinian Muslims and Christians alike hope for a day when they can return, if only for a visit, to a free, independent Palestine.

Ray Hanania

Page at left and above: Palestinian American women reenact the Palestinian pre-wedding Henna Ceremony at a Chicagoland event. Henna is a plant-based, reddish-orange, temporary but long-lasting dye. In preparing the Palestinian woman for marriage, beautiful henna designs are placed on her hands, feet and sometimes around her eyes.

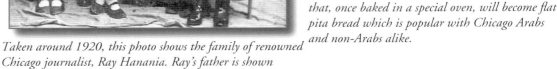

Ray Hanania

Taken around 1920, this photo shows the family of renowned Chicago journalist, Ray Hanania. Ray's father is shown standing, at right, with his family in their Jerusalem home.

Ray Hanania

Ribieh Hussein, a Palestinian from the village of Beitunia, opened one of the first Arab bakeries in Orland Park. Ribieh is pictured kneading dough that, once baked in a special oven, will become flat pita bread which is popular with Chicago Arabs and non-Arabs alike.

111

RAY HANANIA & FAMILY

Growing up in an Arab family on the south side of Chicago near Pill Hill, I have memories of my mother driving and picking fresh grape leaves from forest preserves and trees lining backyards, then putting them in plastic bags to freeze for the winter months.

Stuffed grape leaves are typical of the Levant or Fertile Crescent region of the Middle East and very popular among the Christian and Muslim Arabs. This commonly found vine could be filled with chunks of spiced rice and lamb stuffing that is "liffed" or rolled into the leaf. My mother would stand at the counter and roll each grape leaf by hand, then carefully place it in a pot of lamb chunks or ox tails which served as a base for cooking. It can be backbreaking work, but I learned to make the meal from watching her prepare it often, especially after church or at Christmas or Easter.

In my book, The Arabs of Chicagoland, *I focus on the growing Arab American community. Arabs are known for extending friendship so that newcomers will feel part of the extended family.*

In the old days, it was not easy to find Arabic food ingredients. My mother would ask visiting relatives from the Middle East to bring spices with them. In 1966, Ahmed and Ibrahim Ziyad opened Chicago's first Arab American grocery store. It is a great place for other Arabs to shop or exchange pleasant conversation.

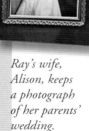

Ray's wife, Alison, keeps a photograph of her parents' wedding.

STUFFED GRAPE LEAVES

INGREDIENTS

200 freshly picked leaves (or two jars of Ziyad Brothers bottled leaves)

2 cups rice, raw

1 12-oz. can diced tomatoes (or 2 large, fresh tomatoes chopped into small chunks)

5 lbs. leg of lamb, diced by hand (or ground at the butcher)

5 lbs. bone-in lamb shank chunks (or 4 lbs. ox tail)

5 cups water

¼ cup olive oil

1 onion, diced

1 tbsp. cumin

4 garlic clove sections, skinned and diced

Rinse grape leaves then place on edge of colander to drip in sink. Mix rice and diced lamb in a bowl. Add olive oil, cumin, diced garlic and ½ of the diced onion. Empty juice from tomatoes into bowl and mix thoroughly.

Place lamb shank chunks in large five-gallon pot. Arrange meat to cover bottom of pot. Fill pot with water to just cover meat. Add remaining diced onions and diced tomato chunks into pot. Begin slow boil of pot, covered, during preparation of grape leaves.

Trim stems from grape leaves. With stem side towards you and tip of leaf pointing away, spread leaf out on rolling table with the dark side of leaf down. Arrange a small chunk of rice/lamb mixture in the center along the leaf's stem. Fold leaf flaps on the right and left over rice/lamb mixture, then roll leaf towards leaf tip until completely rolled. Stack nearby. Continue until all 200 leaves are rolled.

Reduce heat on pot to very low simmer. Place rolled leaves in pot on top of meat one at a time. Insure water level covers meat. Arrange stuffed grape leaves to form several layers. Cover pot, raise flame to low-medium and gently boil for 45 minutes. Check to insure pot has heavy steam inside and does not evaporate water during cooking cycle. Turn off flame. Remove cooked grape leaves one at a time to arrange on a plate. Remove cooked meat and arrange either around the grape leaves or on a separate plate. Ready to serve hot.

SERVES 20

MUSTAFA (STEVE) ADAWI AND FAMILY

Chicago is a melting pot for so many different cultures and cuisines. I love experiencing the abundance of spices, meats and vegetables—unlike that of any other city. I believe I could enjoy eating at a different restaurant every night!

As a youth, I would help my mother in the kitchen. Being very fast with the knife, my mother told me that I have, "gifted hands."

Prior to the 1967 war, I departed Palestine. Traveling and working in Lebanon and Kuwait, I met a head chef named Abu Ramadan. I always watched his hands, becoming a student on the spices he used in cooking. He often told me each spice had a job to do, so I remained curious and attentive.

I eventually moved to the south side of Chicago, opening a restaurant on 63rd Street. In the mid-1970s, I served as one of the chefs for Muhammad Ali. I kept moving west on 63rd as I fell in love with the Chicago Lawn area. Now, I reside in Palos Heights with my wife, Vicky, and my daughter, Ayesha, as we serve Middle Eastern food to our customers at Steve's Shish Kebab.

Making other people happy through the food I serve brings me great satisfaction. I also appreciate my customers' willingness to try new foods which I develop often. As long as they are willing to give my innovative food a try, I am willing to fulfill their requests.

MENSEF
(SAFFRON SAUCE OVER LAMB)

INGREDIENTS

MEAT
12 8-oz. pieces bone-in lamb
 (6 lbs. total)
1 tsp. allspice
½ tsp. cinnamon
4 tsp. salt
1 pinch saffron
1 tsp. black pepper

SAUCE
1 stone of jameed (available at Middle Eastern grocers)
6½ cups water
Pinch of saffron
2 tbsp. cornstarch

RICE
3 cups rice
3 tbsp. corn (or vegetable) oil
1 tsp. salt

GARNISH
3 pieces pita bread, split and opened
1 cup pine nuts (or almonds), toasted
¼ cup parsley, chopped

Wash lamb thoroughly. Add meat to a large pot, cover with water and add all spices. Bring to a boil, cover and reduce heat to a simmer until meat is tender.

Put a pinch of saffron in ½ cup water. Let stand for at least 15-20 minutes until water is a golden color. Strain saffron leaves from the liquid and reserve.

Using a grater, grate the jameed stone and add to the remaining six cups of water. Soak for two hours. Whisk until the stone is dissolved completely. Add a ½ cup of the saffron reserve liquid and two tablespoons cornstarch mixed in four tablespoons water. Blend. Cook on low heat, whisking constantly until hot. Do not boil. Set this finished sauce aside.

Soak rice in hot water for 30 minutes then drain. Add water to at least ¾ inch above the rice. Stir in salt and oil. Bring to a boil. When water has evaporated from the top, lower heat and cover until rice has absorbed liquid. Remove from heat to rest for 15 minutes as it continues to cook.

On a serving plate, arrange pita bread around the bottom. Cover with some of the saffron sauce (until bread is covered) then add rice, smoothing rice into a small mound. Arrange meat on the rice. Cover completely with saffron sauce. Save a small amount of sauce to serve separately. Sprinkle with pine nuts and parsley.

SERVES 6-8

In 966 A.D., the Polish state embraced Christianity thus aligning its interests, then and now, with Western civilization. By the 16th century, the land known as Poland enjoyed a reputation as a center for prosperity, stability, culture and intellectual thought. However, by the 18th century, Poland's increasingly decentralized government weakened the nation to such an extent that its more aggressive neighbors could, and would, literally tear it apart. The Austrian, Prussian and Russian Empires each took pieces of Poland, thrice partitioning the nation into non-existence by 1795. Therefore, when the first Poles entered Chicago in the 1830s, their homeland did not appear on any map. Until the end of World War I and the Treaty of Versailles, Polish immigrants to Chicago did not officially come from Poland, but rather, their documentation read "Prussia," "Russia," "Germany" or "Austro-Hungarian Empire." However, as the Polish immigrants of Chicago would decidedly prove, Poland and its vibrant culture were far from dead.

Though Poles had been entering Chicago at a slow pace beginning in the 1830s, it was not until the end of the Civil War that Poles began to arrive en masse. This immigration wave known as the *Za Chlebem* (For Bread) migration continued steadily until the 1920s, bringing with it hundreds of thousands of Polish peasants, first from the German partition, then later the Russian and Austrian partitions. Many of the *Za Chlebem* immigrants lived in the Polish Triangle at Division,

Dignitaries gather at the base of the Kosciusko Monument after the Polish Constitution Day Parade in 2007.

POLISH

Milwaukee and Ashland. Others earned their living in the steel and meatpacking industries, and settled their families in nearby industrial neighborhoods on the Northwest side, the Near West side, as well as Bridgeport, McKinley Park, Back of the Yards, South Chicago, Pullman and Hegewisch.

The *Za Chlebem* immigrants, almost uniformly Roman Catholic, soon discovered that they had entered a city in which earlier arriving groups, such

as the Germans and Irish, had already gained a strong foothold in trade unions and in the running of the Catholic Archdiocese of Chicago. In fact, early Polish immigrants actually encountered hostility among their fellow Catholics in local parishes who did not wish Polish traditions to be observed. They were, however, welcomed by the Bohemians at St. Adalbert's.

In addition, the decision by Polish workers in the 1880s to become strikebreakers when Irish and German workers were on strike against the meatpacking industry further exacerbated this type of inter-ethnic antagonism.

In response, the Polish immigrants created their own world, their own Polonia, which would become not only a model of immigrant self-sufficiency, but also one of cultural preservation.

In light of the devout nature of the Polish immigrants, one could argue that Polonia began with the founding of the first Polish-centered Chicago parish, St. Stanislaus Kostka in 1867. Peter Kiolbassa further facilitated the building of Polonia by inviting the Polish religious order, the Congregation of the Resurrection, including the Sisters, to minister to the needs of the Polish Catholic community. From there over 60 Polish-centered Catholic parishes would be built, each becoming a micro-center for the Polish community. Moreover, the Resurrectionists, as they came to be called, also founded local Catholic secondary schools that would educate generations of Polish Catholics and other local Chicagoans.

Community self-sufficiency and cultural preservation would also be aided by the work of Polish-centered female religious orders, established in Poland, such as the Felician Sisters, the Franciscan Sisters of Blessed Kunegunda and by the Sisters of the Holy Family of Nazareth. Members of each of these orders taught thousands of Polish American children in Chicago, in both Polish and English, with the dual goals of preparing these children for life in America while at the same time preserving Polish culture within the community.

The Polish community also addressed its own societal needs when the Sisters of the Holy Family of Nazareth opened a hospital for the Polish community in 1894, officially named St. Mary of Nazareth, but also known as The Polish Hospital.

Members of the Polish community organized a home for the elderly in 1898, and an orphanage in 1910. Further, the Polonia-founded Polish Welfare Association provided various social services of the community, while St. Adalbert Cemetery, established by members of the Polish and Czech communities in 1872, and Resurrection Cemetery, opened in 1904, gave Polonia final resting places.

A view of Milwaukee Avenue, the center of commercial Polonia, looking northwest from Ashland Avenue, circa 1910.

As for the economy of Polonia, along with the income received from industry, within Polonia existed a strong entrepreneurial class, comprised of men and women who opened businesses and served fellow Poles along Milwaukee, Archer, Ashland, Commercial Avenues and Division and West 47th Streets. The Polonia commercial areas would eventually become so developed with shops, businesses, restaurants and professional offices that many Polish Chicagoans of the late 19th and early 20th centuries never really had to leave their neighborhood. In fact, Polonia brought Polish issues and culture right into the home with their many Polish-language newspapers and publications.

However, the *Za Chlebem* immigrants were not satisfied to create merely a neighborhood-level Polonia, as dramatically shown by their community's creation of major fraternal organizations. The latter still serve hundreds of thousands of Polish Americans across America today, while remaining headquartered in Chicago. In addition to addressing the insurance needs of the Polish community, the fraternals also played a major role in preserving Polish culture and in working for freedom and prosperity in their native homeland. The first major fraternal, the Polish Roman Catholic Union of America (PRCUA), started in 1873. In its efforts to retain Polish culture in America and to liberate Poland, the PRCUA stressed the Catholicism of the Polish people. Though having the same general goals of the PRCUA, the Polish National Alliance (PNA), founded in 1880, emphasized Polish nationalism and made the Polish independence its first priority. This diversity of emphasis unfortunately led to periods of antagonism between the two fraternals. Finally, after being denied entry into both the PRCUA and the PNA for reasons of gender, a group of Polish women, under the leadership of Stefania Chmielinska, responded in true Polish fashion by founding their own fraternal, the Polish Women's Alliance, in 1898.

With the coming of the 20th century and World War I, the Chicago Polonia community worked tirelessly, under the leadership of the major fraternals, to free Poland from its foreign occupiers. Their efforts were rewarded when Poland regained its independence in the aftermath of World War I. In the years following, Polish immigration to Chicago dropped off markedly due not only to Polish independence, but also to new laws enacted by Congress in the 1920s that severely restricted immigration.

As of September 1, 1939, the day Adolf Hitler's Nazi forces invaded Poland, thereby launching World War II, the fate of Chicago's Polonia would be dramatically altered again. Enduring six years of vicious Nazi control, Poland emerged in 1945 with six million of its people dead, an economy in ruins and Joseph Stalin's Red Army occupying its territory. As if all that unfathomable tragedy had not been enough, and despite all the efforts Chicago's Polonia undertook to assist their Polish brethren by shipping millions of pounds of supplies and lobbying Congress and the White House for Polish territorial integrity, Poland lost one-third of her land and would become a satellite state for the Soviet Union, in accordance with an agreement reached between the United States, Great Britain and the Soviet Union.

The end of World War II initiated a new wave of Polish immigrants to Chicago, the émigrés, a group mostly comprised of people displaced by the events of World War II and the subsequent Communist takeover of Poland. Largely middle class and professional in background, the émigrés brought new vigor to what had been an increasingly Americanized Polonia. They also brought with them the passion to liberate Poland, and for approximately the next four decades, the émigrés of Polonia were focused on liberating Poland from Communist control.

The anti-Communist efforts within Polonia were immeasurably enhanced in the early 1980s by the actions of their courageous relatives in Poland, particularly Lech Walesa and those fighting within the Solidarity movement that he founded. Though the Communists cracked down on Solidarity by declaring martial law in 1981, Pandora's Box had already been opened. The Polish people wanted freedom, and they were willing to fight and even die to get it. In the end, factions of the Solidarity movement, which recently arrived in Chicago, played a major role in the fall of the Soviet Empire, and Chicago's Polonia was there every step of the way, giving support, sending money and lobbying Congress and the President.

The events surrounding the Solidarity movement and the collapse of the Soviet Union proved to be a catalyst for another wave of Polish immigration to Chicago, in that since the early 1980s, hundreds of thousands of Poles have arrived in Chicago. This group, known as New Polonia, is upwardly mobile and is comprised of many artists, intellectuals, professionals and entrepreneurs. New Polonia has greatly enriched Chicago by both reviving old cultural institutions and opening new ones within Polonia, and by opening businesses that serve the whole of Chicago.

Indeed, each of the three waves of Polish immigrants to Chicago has proven themselves remarkably adept at preserving and promoting their Polish heritage, even at times when Poland did not officially exist or when it was not free. It is as if the tragedies that have befallen Poland during the past two centuries forced the Polish people to ask themselves the question, "What is Polish?" In the process of answering, Chicago's Polonia realized that being Polish was not restricted to some area of land in Eastern Europe. It is tradition. It is language. It is the song in your heart. Polonia is where you make it.

Polish sausage was, and is, one of Polonia's most recognized products.

Count Casimir Pulaski, hero of the American Revolution, is known throughout Chicago.

Popular polka musician, L'il Wally Jagiello.

Above left: PNA (Polish National Alliance) officials greet a group of Polish displaced persons in 1949.

Above right: Home of the Polish Museum of America and the Polish Roman Catholic Union of America, founded in 1873.

Left: Polish Constitution Day Parade float in 1982.

Right: Organized in 1867, St. Stanislaus Kostka Church had 40,000 members by the year 1899.

WIGILIA (POLISH CHRISTMAS EVE DINNER)

Wesolych Swiat Bozego Narodzenia; that is the way to say "Merry Christmas" in Polish. It is then that the "Wigilia" (Christmas Eve dinner) is served. After the "Oplatek" (traditional wafer) is broken, the family enjoys mushroom soup, "sledzie" (pickled herring), fried fish, pierogi, beans, sauerkraut, cabbage rolls, dried fruit compote and assorted pastries.

Both photos by Stanley Wlodkowski

Swieconka (Polish Easter Meal)

Swieconka is the name for the Easter meal. On Holy Thursday, the
women and girls begin coloring Easter eggs. A cake in the shape of
a "Baranek" (Pascal Lamb) is baked and adorned with a banner
symbolizing Christ's victory over death. Ham, sausage, salt, vinegar
and "barszcz" (borscht soup) are included in the meal.

DOBRA BIELINSKI

After graduating from the University of Illinois with an M.A. in U.S. Foreign Policy, I suddenly realized I wanted to be a chef. In 1998, my mother, Stasia Hawryszczuk (photo above, at right), and I opened up a bakery, Delightful Pastries, in Jefferson Park. Though my roots are Polish, there was a learning curve in discovering how to make traditional pastries. Initially, I had to correspond with bakers in Poland and had books shipped to me so that I could bake Polish cakes and tortes. We make authentic pastries by using quality ingredients that shine through and speak for themselves.

When I visited my cousin, Eleanor, in Silesia, Poland, she baked this cheesecake recipe for me. I fell in love with it and brought it back to Chicago. I chose peaches for the recipe but other regions in the "old country" use cherries, apples and, in the wintertime, raisins and candied orange peel.

In Jefferson Park, we have created a bond with the locals. Our customers know us and we know them. We provide quality in our authentic European pastries and they provide support. To live in Chicago means to be truly multi-ethnic and exposed to the many nationalities living here—certainly a great way to expand one's culinary and cultural horizons.

PEACH CHEESECAKE

DOUGH	BATTER
1 4-oz. stick butter, chilled	8 oz. sugar
¾ cup sugar	5.5 oz. egg yolks
2 cups all-purpose flour	2 oz. custard powder (or cornstarch)
1 tsp. baking powder	2.2 lbs. farmer's cheese
1 egg	1 tsp. vanilla extract
1 egg yolk	1 tsp. orange extract
	1 tsp. lemon extract
	6.5 oz. egg whites
	3.5 oz. sugar
	1 16-oz. can sliced peaches

Dough: In an electric mixer fitted with a paddle, cream together butter, sugar and eggs. Add baking powder and flour; mixing until it comes together. Remove dough from mixing bowl and knead slightly by hand. Roll out dough into a 13"x 9"x 2" pan lined with parchment paper. Bake at 350F for 25-30 minutes until dough is golden color

Batter: Align drained peaches on the cooled dough, keeping them ¾ inch from the edges. Spray sides of pan with non-stick spray. In an electric mixer fitted with a paddle, mix egg yolks, custard powder, sugar and extracts for ten minutes starting out at low speed, increasing to high speed. Add the cheese and mix well. Empty contents into a large bowl, then thoroughly clean mixing bowl.

In an electric mixer fitted with a whisk, whip egg whites and, when volume has increased, add 3.5 ounces of sugar. Continue whisking until medium stiff peaks are reached. Gently fold egg whites into the cheese batter. Pour batter into the cake pan, smoothing out the top. Bake for 60-90 minutes until a paring knife inserted comes out clean. When cooled, sift with powdered sugar and serve.

SERVES 12

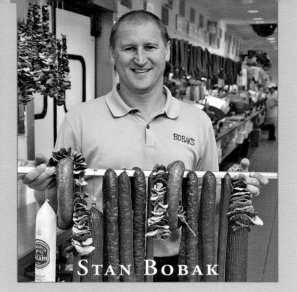

STAN BOBAK

My family came from the Polish Highland Region. I met my wife at a Polish folklore dance group in Chicago. Born and raised in the Polish community, I attended the language school and grew with the Bobak Sausage Company. This has given me a sense of heritage I now pass on to my children. Handing down recipes that have been in the Bobak family for generations is an integral part of that heritage.

There is a Polish saying; "Jedzcie, pijcie i popuszczajcie pasa" (Eat, drink and loosen your belt). The "bigos" (meat stew) was a must after the hunt and was often considered the national dish of Poland. Said to have been introduced by Wladislaus II, a Lithuanian prince who became king in 1385, it's been a classic dish for centuries. Our family version includes smoked sausage and heavy wood-smoked bacon as well as a unique mix of spices, which makes bigos one of my favorite dishes.

Committed to my Polish roots, I have participated in the Polish Constitution Day May 3rd Parade, Taste of Polonia and Taste of Chicago as well as sponsoring various Polish organizations and supporting a number of schools and events. Although not a chef, I am a "food connoisseur" so it is important that we, the Bobak Sausage Company, diversify into different ethnic markets since diversity is what Chicago is all about.

124

BIGOS
(HUNTERS' STEW)

INGREDIENTS

2-2.5 lbs. sauerkraut

½ lb. boneless pork

½ lb. veal

½ lb. sausage

¼ lb. slab bacon

¼ oz. dry mushrooms (soaked in cold water for 30 minutes)

2 oz. fatback

1 large onion, chopped

½ cup red wine (optional)

1 tbsp. flour

Salt

Ground pepper

Sugar

Finely chop sauerkraut, scald with boiling water and cook together with mushrooms (after soaking) for about one hour. Rinse, salt and fry meat together with diced fatback. Add cooked meats to sauerkraut together with slab of bacon, add wine (optional) then cook for 40 minutes until tender. Take out meat, slab of bacon and mushrooms then dice them and return to stew. Remove skin from sausage, slice sausage and add to stew.

In a small pan, gently brown onions until transparent. Add flour and mix with one tablespoon of water, then add to stew. Bring the stew to a boil, then lower heat to simmer. Add salt, pepper and sugar to taste.

Note: You may add different kinds of meat to the stew (such as leftover roast meat, game or poultry). Bigos is very tasty when reheated.

SERVES 8

DOMINIQUE WILK

PHEASANT IN ROSEMARY AND SAGE CREAM SAUCE

INGREDIENTS

1 pheasant, cut in quarters
1 cup chicken stock
1 cup cold heavy whipping cream
1 tsp. flour
1 tbsp. fresh sage, chopped

MARINADE

1 cup olive oil
4 garlic cloves, crushed
½ tsp. red sweet pepper
Bunch of fresh rosemary
Bunch of fresh sage
Salt and freshly ground pepper to taste

When my mother (photo opposite page) was not creating wonderful couturier dress designs, she was cooking the pheasant, wild boar, quail and bear my father hunted. Hunting is part of my ancestry but I am the first crossover, the first female of my family to join the men. My husband and I have hunted in Africa for game like the kudu, zebra and impala. There, hunting is more like the "old country."

Hunting in Poland is a religious experience. In the U.S., you buy a license and shoot prey which has often been released from breeding farms. But in the deep woods of Poland, we focus on the blessing from the patron saint of hunters, St. Hubert. The shot must be guaranteed perfect so it won't maim the noble creature. We always killed for the family table, not for sport, and were taught never to waste anything.

In Poland, around the 15th and 16th centuries, it was the exclusive right of kings and nobility to hunt since they owned the land. Peasants would be killed if caught poaching, but later the laws relaxed

so they could hunt pheasants and rabbits.

In our family, my brother married a Polish American girl and immigrated to Chicago. My father, after my mother's death, and I soon followed. Chicago is such an exceptional city. With its Polish restaurants, churches, language and social life, sometimes I feel like I'm in Poland. I never feel a separation from my homeland as its wonderful traditions have continued on. Today, I try to preserve my family heritage by both hunting and cooking game.

Combine all marinade ingredients then marinate pheasant pieces overnight. Remove pheasant pieces and reserve the marinade.

Brown pheasant pieces in a non-stick skillet over high heat. Add marinade and chicken stock, then cover and cook over medium heat until pheasant is done. Remove pheasant pieces, rosemary and sage. Strain the liquid.

Stir flour into cold heavy whipping cream, then gradually add in reserved cooking liquid until a creamy sauce is obtained. Adjust seasonings to taste.

Return pheasant pieces to the sauce then simmer for 5-10 minutes.

Finally, sprinkle with fresh sage and serve.

SERVES 4

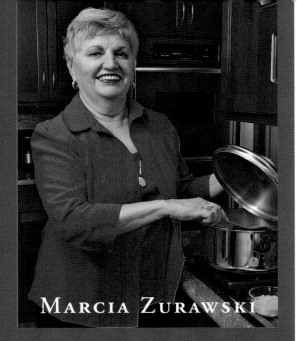

MARCIA ZURAWSKI

BIALY BARSZCZ
(WHITE BORSCHT)

INGREDIENTS

6 cups stock reserved from cooking one
    pair of Polish sausages (approx. 1½
    to 2 lbs. in weight)

2 tbsp. white horseradish

2 tbsp. vinegar

1 tsp. salt

¾ cup water

2 tbsp. sour cream

4 tbsp. flour

3–4 hard-boiled eggs, thinly sliced

Fill a large stock pot with two quarts water. Place a pair of Polish sausage links in the water. Bring to a boil. Reduce heat then simmer for about an hour. Remove sausage links to a platter to cool, then cut into thin slices.

Bring six cups of the sausage stock, horseradish, vinegar and salt to a boil, then lower heat and simmer.

While waiting for the stock to come to a boil, in a small bowl whisk together ¾ cup water, sour cream and flour. Gradually add this mixture to the simmering soup. To ensure a smooth texture, pass the sour cream mixture through a strainer directly into the soup. It will take only a short time to thicken.

After the soup has thickened, add the thinly sliced Polish sausage and eggs to the soup until heated through. Season to taste.

SERVES 4

*Marcia and her mother,
Sophie Magiera.*

Although I am not a chef, I do enjoy making foods gleaned from my family's heritage. One of my favorites is bialy barszcz, a traditional Polish soup served at Easter. The recipe was from my grandmother, who met and married my grandfather in Chicago.

My "busia" (grandmother), who once lived in a farming community outside of Krakow, was the one who, thankfully, re-created this recipe for her family in the United States. I had the opportunity to visit busia's family homestead during the 1960s and found it very interesting to learn how all the farmers lived in a row of homes. They rode out each morning to tend to their tract of land then returned at the end of the day.

Busia and "dziatki" (grandfather) came to Chicago to build a better life for themselves. Starting their married life in an apartment, their goal was to own their own home where they could raise their four children—Marie, Sophie, Evelyn and Henry. For Polish people, ownership of land was an indication that one had "arrived" and achieved success in America.

I remember Busia and Dziatki Lakoma would often entertain their numerous immigrant friends and relatives on Sundays. A large portion of the visit was devoted to serving a great meal filled with traditional Polish foods. This Polish trait of hospitality is a tradition carried on by recent immigrants and descendants of immigrants who live in the Chicago area.

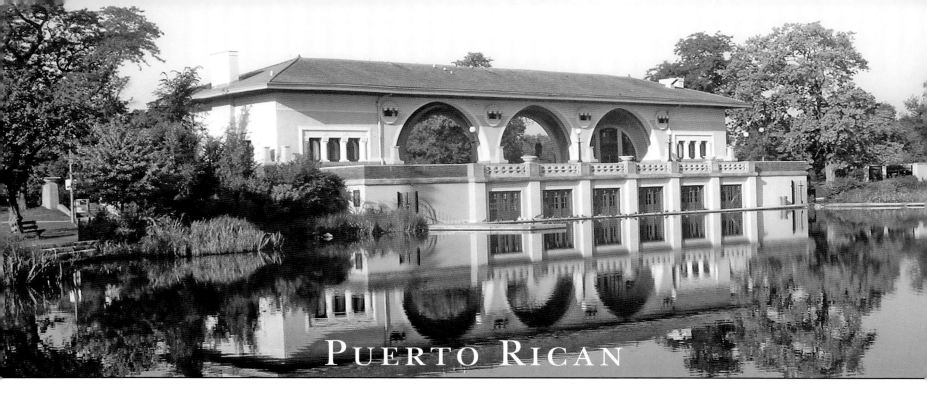

PUERTO RICAN

When Congress passed the Jones Act of 1917, it granted United States citizenship to any Puerto Rican born in either the United States or on the island of Puerto Rico. Therefore, when native Puerto Ricans arrived in Chicago in the late 1940s, they began the uniquely Puerto Rican journey of "citizen immigrant." Whereas other group migrations to Chicago during the second half of the twentieth century would always be subject to the immigration policy whims of Congress, the Puerto Rican immigrant could always move back and forth from the island to the mainland as often as his or her pocketbook would allow. Yet, because Puerto Ricans born on the island spoke Spanish instead of English, in many ways these immigrants, the early arrivals in particular, seemed as "foreign" as if they had just stepped off a ship that had left port at Buenos Aires.

Large-scale Puerto Rican immigration to Chicago began in 1946, when representatives of the employment agency of Castle, Barton and Associates, a Chicago-based firm, traveled to Puerto Rico to recruit women for domestic service and men for unskilled foundry labor in the Chicagoland area.

The early Puerto Rican immigrants lived in neighborhoods throughout the city, but by the 1960s, the Puerto Rican population had concentrated in Lincoln Park, West Town and Humboldt Park. Yet, their presence in Lincoln Park was not to last past the mid-1960s, when redevelopment programs displaced Puerto Rican families, who generally moved to West Town and Humboldt Park. This tight concentration of the community allowed for the creation along Division Street (or *la Division*, as the residents call it) of Chicago's first barrio.

La Division played host to the first annual Puerto Rican Parade, a celebration of ethnic pride which grew out of *Dia de San Juan* (Saint John's Day) religious festivities sponsored by *Los Caballeros de San Juan* (The Knights of Saint John), one of the first organizations founded by Puerto Ricans in Chicago.

Sadly, the first Puerto Rican Parade, dated June 12, 1966, ended in a riot that lasted two days. The event was the result of a police shooting of a local Puerto Rican man. Like many of the riots of the 1960s, this one opened the eyes of the nation to the poverty and discrimination suffered by the Puerto Rican community. It also revealed the poor relations between that population and the Chicago police department.

Within weeks of the riot, the Chicago Commission on Human Relations held open hearings in which the serious needs and concerns of the Puerto Rican community could be voiced. Moreover, in the years following, Puerto Ricans formed community-action groups that kept Puerto Rican educational, healthcare, housing, employment and civil rights concerns on the minds

Opposite page: The boathouse in beautiful Lombard Park, the heart of Puerto Rican Chicago. Efforts are also underway to restore and record the historic park stables.

Men of the Vazquez family, Leonzio, Alberto, Sr., Alberto, Jr. and Omar, pose under one of two giant flags that announce the entrance to Paseo Boricua.

Popular entertainer Giovanni Serrano keeps the Latin beat as Sonia Lopez provides encouragement.

Wilmarie Ayala presents a unique display of the Puerto Rican and American colors at the Festival Queen event.

of city politicians.

Despite that tumultuous first Puerto Rican Parade, *la Division* remains a major center for the community. At both the intersection of Division and Western, and the intersection of Division and California, flies a massive Puerto Rican flag. Inbetween these flags is the *Paseo Boricua* (Puerto Rican Road), where the spirit of the island can be found in every shop and restaurant.

In addition, though *la Division* is still a popular place of residence for immigrants from Puerto Rico, many members of Chicago's Puerto Rican community have moved to other city neighborhoods such as Belmont-Cragin, Hermosa and Logan Square, and suburban areas such as Schaumburg and Naperville. As of the 2000 census, 113,055 of Puerto Rican descent lived in Chicago, making the community, which comprises 15% of the total Latino population, the second largest Latino group in Chicago.

In recent years members of the community have made strong inroads into the fast-growing fields of consulting and information technology. In an economic landscape in which the world seems to grow a little smaller everyday, the unique perspective of the bilingual citizen immigrant is more valuable than ever.

Puerto Rican musical celebrities in Chicago, about to play at the Puerto Rican Festival, stop by Victor "Papa" and Nancy Garcia's restaurant on Division to enjoy the authentic Puerto Rican fare.

All photographs in the Puerto Rican chapter are by Luis Cabrera of Face Photo.

Above: The Souchet Juice Bar, famous for its piña coladas, has been in the park for many years.
At left: DJ Ramiro Lopez sits behind and encourages a budding star of the stage.

A treasured image for any Puerto Rican family.

The Puerto Rican Festival attracts large crowds every year.

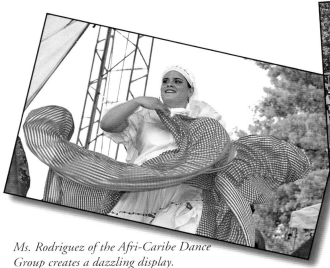

Ms. Rodriguez of the Afri-Caribe Dance Group creates a dazzling display.

The Festival features colorful booths that not only offer Puerto Rican souvenirs but items from many other Latin and South American countries.

Above: A stylish photo of (left to right) Miss Teen Puerto Rico Jackie Medina, Puerto Rican Parade Committee of Chicago Queen Yesenia Rodriguez and 1st Princess Sandra I. Perez.

A great day for a parade. Left to right are Alderman Ariel Reboyras, Commissioner Norma Reyes, local McDonald's owner Juan Mendez, Senator Iris Y. Martinez, Commissioner Roberto Maldanado, Commissioner Joe Barrios, Mayor Richard Daley, President P.R.P.C.C. Miguel Sanchez, Representative William Delgado and Leonzio Vazquez.

PETER FIGUEROA

I was raised watching my mother and grandmother prepare one of their favorite meals, "arroz con gandules" (rice with pigeon peas), enhanced with a combination of Caribbean flavors. In Puerto Rico, this is a traditional side dish served at most festivals with a Puerto Rican version of Mexican tamales.

My family came to Chicago in three waves. My oldest brothers came first; my little brothers and I came next; and my mother came last. Over the years, I started adding my own ingredients to this family recipe. Even though I do not have any culinary education, my father developed his cooking skills the same way. It was the beginning of my interest in cooking and making foods from my homeland. Like my father before me, a spirit of creativity inspired me to experiment.

Since 1990, I have been working at my North California Street restaurant Borinquen, home of "El Jibarito" (a sandwich combination of beefsteak and fried green plantain). Initially, I worked fifteen-hour days making sure the restaurant was successful. As business continued to flourish, I called my father in Puerto Rico and asked him to come help me grow my business.

"Papa Juan" eventually answered the call and we have been working together ever since providing our customers with food they enjoy. In its own small way, our restaurant is an example of how Puerto Rican food has been a positive influence on the culinary atmosphere across Chicago and the nation at large.

ROASTED PORK AND RICE WITH PIGEON PEAS

PORK

10-12 lbs. pork leg

14 garlic cloves (7 to be crushed; 7 kept whole for stuffing)

½ cup corn oil

1 tbsp. salt

1 tbsp. pepper

4 bay leaves

4 packets sazon (pre-packaged coriander and annatto seasonings)

RICE

4 cups water

2 cups long grain rice

1 can pigeon peas

4 oz. tomato sauce

½ cup corn oil

½ lb. cooked ham

¼ cup green peppers

¼ cup onions, diced

¼ cup cilantro and reca (culatro)

1 tbsp. garlic, crushed

4 bay leaves

2 packets sazon

2 packets dry ham (½ oz. packages)

1 tbsp. red artificial coloring

Salt to taste

1 tsp. white vinegar

2 tbsp. sofrito (Spanish seasoning found in specialty grocery store)

PORK: Grind and combine seasoning ingredients, except seven whole garlic cloves. Poke holes in pork leg and insert seven garlic cloves. Rub ground seasonings on the pork leg. Place in baking pan and cover with aluminum foil, then bake at 350 degrees for two hours. Remove aluminum foil and bake uncovered for an additional 1½ hours until desired crispness of pork skin.

RICE: Combine all ingredients (except rice) in a cooking pot then heat on medium until boiling. Add rice and cook for 10-15 minutes until ingredients begin to dry. Reduce heat to low setting. Cover and cook for an additional 40 minutes, stirring occasionally.

SERVES 8-12

SOUTH ASIANS

The South Asians of Chicago come from a land that many peoples have invaded, but none could fully conquer. One of the cradles of civilization, the people of this region lived in cities built according to precise mathematics, communicated via a sophisticated written language, stored food in granaries and even had running toilets in their homes as early as 3000 B.C. This society, known as the Indus Valley Civilization, lasted until approximately 1500 B.C., at which time the first of many invaders, the Aryans, arrived. The latter settled in the north of what was to be known as India and brought with them the Sanskrit language, the caste system and cultural traditions which are still a strong part of South Asian culture today.

From approximately 500 B.C. until the 19th century, India endured invasions, some violent, from the Persians, Greeks, Arabs, Mongols, Portuguese and British. Each group made their mark on India, bringing knowledge, religious beliefs, languages and systems of government. But none made India

136

their own, as local kingdoms always survived in one way or another and as the people of South Asia persevered, living their lives according to their own traditions and beliefs.

Indeed, even the British, who exerted control over India for over 300 years; first via the East India Company and then, after 1858, through a sophisticated bureaucratic system known as the Raj, could not keep India in their grasp forever. Under the Raj, India became a major source of profit for the British. It was, however, not a fortune they were willing to share with the native South Asian residents, who were generally treated as second-class citizens.

But India survived and it would do so by its own terms. Under the extraordinary leadership of Mahatma Gandhi, the various religious and ethnic groups of India united as one, and brought the well-armed British Raj to its knees through a revolutionary form of action, the peaceful protest.

The British left India in 1947. In that same

year, India officially divided into two nations, Pakistan, which is majority Muslim, and India, which is majority Hindu.

Yet, as recently as the early 1960s, very few South Asians resided in Chicago, or the United States for that matter. However, in little more than a generation, the Indian and Pakistani communities have made a tremendously positive impact on their new home.

For much of the 20th century, South Asians were denied admission to the United States under the Barred Zone Act of 1917, which forbade several Asian groups, including South Asians, from immigrating to or becoming citizens of the United States. Indians received some legal relief in 1923 when Congress permitted citizenship to Indians, who were considered British subjects as the Raj was in force during that era. Nevertheless, it was not until congressional passage of the Immigration and Nationality Act of 1965, which greatly relaxed federal rules, that a large number of Pakistanis and

Indians came to the Chicago shoreline. These early arrivals, mostly male professionals and graduate students, gifted Chicago with their intelligence, drive, commitment to education and incredible work ethic. These men served Chicago as doctors, scientists, engineers, managers and computer professionals; all roles in which their sons and daughters still perform for their fellow Chicagoans today.

In the years following the initial wave of South Asian immigration, the families of these professionals joined their loved ones, thereby greatly increasing the local South Asian population. Recent decades have brought not only working class citizens, but also very entrepreneurial Indians and Pakistanis who have opened shops, gas stations, and restaurants all over Chicago, but particularly along Devon Avenue.

In the "Little India" section of Devon Avenue, one can find ingredients for every curry imaginable, lovely strands and bangles of gold, and the latest Bollywood sensation among its theatres and video stores. To celebrate the vibrancy of this community, the City of Chicago renamed the portion of Devon Avenue bordering Little India *Gandhi Marg* (Gandhi Way), in honor of Mahatma Gandhi, the founder of India.

Equally lively and culturally rich is the Pakistani section of Devon Avenue, renamed Mohammed Ali Jinnah Way, in honor of Pakistan's founder and first governor general. There one can dine on a delicious meal at any of the many restaurants and shop in a menagerie of vibrant color among the many shops. And on August 14th, the locals celebrate the national independence day of Pakistan in a lively parade on Mohammed Ali Jinnah Way.

On the following day, August 15th, the residents of Little India celebrate India's national independence day on *Gandhi Marg*. Despite the tensions that exist between their respective homelands, the Indian and Pakistani Americans of Devon Avenue not only coexist, they thrive.

Nothing exemplifies this cultural pride and the success of the Pakistanis and Indians more than the institutions these communities have built. Mosques, Hindu temples, Sikh *gurudwaras* and Jain temples dot the Chicago landscape, while hundreds of local organizations keep the cultural, social and religious traditions of Pakistan and India alive.

But perhaps the best example of South Asian success can be found in their children, who attend and graduate from universities all over the United States in numbers that dwarf those of many other groups. Indeed, the commitment to education found among the early South Asian arrivals lives on, and Chicago is certainly the better for it.

Jay Morthland

Jay Morthland

South Asian Friendship Center

South Asian Friendship Center

Top left: Sikh musicans perform at many functions.

Above: Joyous celebration on India Independence Day.

Left: Indian American women proudly carrying the flag of India during the India Independence Day Parade on Devon Avenue, the center of Chicago's South Asian community.

Pakistani children join in the festivities.

Rohini Dey, (standing in photo), owner of Vermilion: *I am the concept-originator of this eclectic Indian Latin restaurant. I chose the name Vermilion because it connotes the essence and ebullience of the Indian and Latin American peoples and also overtly celebrates the strength and beauty of femininity. I deliberately steered away from the stereotypes associated with Indian restaurants in America (greasy overspiced fare, sitar muzak, tired visuals and the omnipresent $8 all-you-can-eat buffet with the same 10 items). I founded Vermilion as an antithesis to the norm. We celebrate urbane Indian culture through not only our cuisine, but also the sensual photography we display. In addition, Vermilion offers a selection of authentic regional Indian cuisine (Hyderabadi, Kashmiri, Bombay street foods, Rajasthani, Kerala in the past, Dhaba - current Indian truck-stop fare).*

I received a Master's in Economics from the Delhi School of Economics and came to the U.S. for my Ph.D. in Management Science. Motherhood was in parallel with going entrepreneurial; founding and launching Vermilion was in tandem with the birth of our second daughter, which preceded the opening by a few weeks!

With my executive chef, Maneet Chauhan (seated in photo at left), we are delighted to be at the forefront of fleshing out the unique fusion cuisine of Vermilion. Maneet actually began her culinary career at the WelcomGroup Graduate School of Hotel Administration, India's top hotel management school, followed by internships at India's finest hotels and kitchens. She also attended the foremost culinary school in the U.S., The Culinary Institute of America, Hyde Park. She is extremely passionate about cooking and thrives on working in a creative, challenging and dynamic environment. I interviewed and conducted tastings with over 40 chefs, and Maneet's comfort with innovation made her a natural candidate to take on the challenge of the Latin Indian fusion pioneered at Vermilion.

MIRIS SRI LANKAN SNAPPER

Blend all ingredients for the marinade, then pour over a cleaned and scored snapper. Boil broth until reduced by half. Place marinated snapper into a baking pan then pour in three ladles of broth. Cook snapper at 500 degrees for 30-35 minutes.

Garnish with chopped cilantro, orange zest and serve hot with rice. For a milder and less spicy version, cut back on the red chile powder.

SERVES 1-2

INGREDIENTS

1 1-lb. snapper

MARINADE

5 red chiles
1 tsp. tamarind paste
2 garlic cloves
1 tbsp. fresh ginger, chopped
5 peppercorns
1 tsp. curry powder
Salt
2 tsp. coriander seeds
¼ cup fresh cilantro
2 cinnamon sticks
1 stick lemongrass
¼ cup lime juice

BROTH

2 qts. water
5 stalks curry leaves
1 stalk lemongrass
2 Indian cinnamon sticks
1 tsp. turmeric powder
¼ cup ginger slices
¼ cup cilantro
¼ cup shallots
¼ cup garlic, sliced
¼ cup jalapeno, sliced

2 tbsp. sugar
1 tbsp. curry powder
½ cup lime juice
2 tbsp. tamarind paste
10 whole red chiles, soaked in
    hot water and blended
    with cinnamon sticks
¼ cup paprika
1 tbsp. red chile powder
1 tbsp. salt

RASAM

INGREDIENTS

2 tbsp. sesame oil

½ tsp. cumin (whole)

½ tsp. black mustard (whole)

½ tsp. turmeric powder

1 tsp. black peppercorns (whole)

1 square-inch ginger, minced finely

2 sprigs curry leaves

1 lb. chopped tomatoes (Roma tomatoes
    preferred)

2 tsp. tamarind paste (or substitute with the
    juice of 1 large lemon or 2 small limes)

4 cups water

10–15 sprigs fresh cilantro, roughly chopped

Salt to taste

KANTHA & TARA SHELKE

As an emigrant to Chicago from South India, I have come to benefit from both cultures. To this day, I thoroughly enjoy eating food from my family's native region. At times when I was in college in Fargo, North Dakota, finding the ingredients with an Indian origin was difficult, if not impossible.

Fortunately, I never lost my interest in Indian food as I've been able to share it with my daughter (photo above, at right). One of my favorites is rasam. If chicken soup soothes the soul of Americans, rasam does the same for the people of India. I personally believe it is even more calming for someone, alone in a foreign land, nostalgically longing for their mother's home cooking.

I always thought my mother made the best rasam in the entire world. Dating back to the seventh century, rasam is a part of the daily meal ritual in my homeland, just like soup is on a cold, snowy day in Chicago.

Historically, rasam is prepared with black pepper and tamarind, ingredients both native to and abundant in Tamil Nadu (formerly known as Madras). Tart and spicy tastes penetrate the cuisines of South India as is the case with the flavorful rasam. The tartness comes from tamarind, lemons or limes and the pungent heat (spice) is from the black pepper.

Rasam continues to be prepared on a daily basis in most South Indian households around the world. Of course, the rasam is unique to each family even if the same ingredients are used. It will hold the distinct character and imprint of its cook which gives it an unbeatable nostalgia.

And, with the State of Illinois having the fifth largest population of Indian people, there is little wonder why this type of food has become so popular in Chicago. For me, it's the best of both worlds; enjoying my heritage in an American city that I love!

Heat oil in a large pot over medium heat. Add cumin and mustard seeds which will pop gently. Add peppercorn, turmeric, ginger and curry leaves. Stir for two minutes. Add tomatoes, tamarind paste (or juice substitute) and four cups water; bring to a boil. Cover and simmer for 10-15 minutes. Add cilantro in last five minutes. Salt to taste. Serve alone or over freshly cooked rice. Garnish with a sliver of butter, a sprig of cilantro or a ½ teaspoon of ghee.

SERVES 4

141

Between 1845 and 1930, over one million Swedes immigrated to the United States. In fact, by 1910, one-fifth of all native-born Swedes lived in America. Driven to leave their Scandinavian home by overpopulation, a lack of available farmland, and a late-arriving Swedish Industrial Revolution, the Swedes braved the North Atlantic for an America with fertile lands vast beyond imagination and an exploding economy in which everyone could find work.

In their first two decades of immigration, Swedes came to Chicago as a stop-over city on their way to the black soil of the Great Plains. However, upon arriving in the young Chicago, many decided to forego the life of a farmer and to take advantage of the vital job market of the fast-growing city.

The women were employed as domestic servants. Many of the men, at first, worked on the Illinois and Michigan Canal, and later, worked in skilled and semi-skilled jobs in construction, metalworking, and for companies like McCormack Reaper Works, the Union Stock Yard and the Pullman Palace Car Company.

Starting in the 1880s, the Swedish population of Chicago expanded more than 200%. Attracted by the city's seemingly endless economic growth, these new immigrants helped make Chicago the largest Swedish community in America.

Over the next 50 years Swedes settled in neighborhoods throughout the city. On the North Side, Swedes made a home in Lake View, Andersonville and North Park, while on the West Side, Austin and Belmont Cragin became the place of residence for many Swedish families. As for the South Side, Swedes settled in Hyde Park, Woodlawn, Englewood, West Englewood, South Shore, Greater Grand Crossing, East Side, Morgan Park and Roseland. These neighborhoods often tended to be areas where Germans, Irish and Norwegians settled as well, thereby showing a level of kinship with the ethnic groups who immigrated to Chicago at the same time the Swedes did.

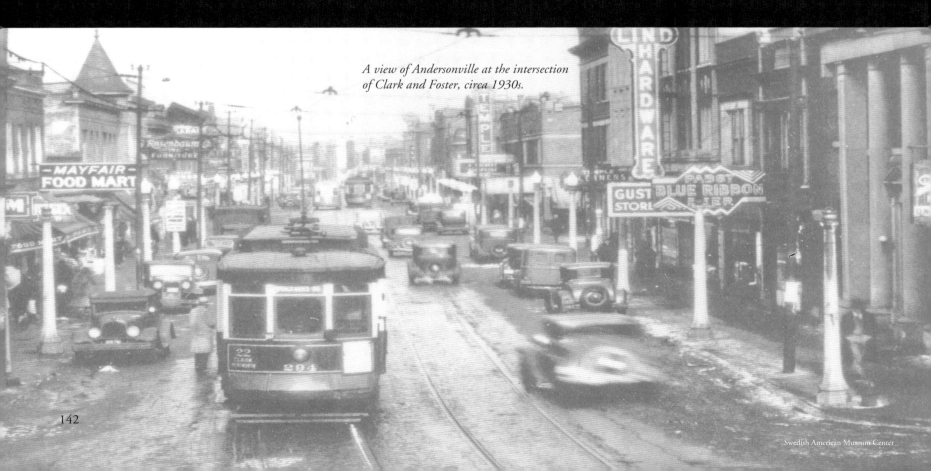

A view of Andersonville at the intersection of Clark and Foster, circa 1930s.

The May Pole event outside the Swedish American Museum Center on Clark Street.

Swedish American Museum Center

Throughout the entire period of Swedish immigration the arriving individuals generally originated from rural, southern Sweden and tended to be young and vigorous, a follower of a Protestant denomination, and literate.

The Protestant culture of the Swedes led them to found several churches such as St. Ansgarius Church in 1849, and Immanuel Lutheran Church in 1853. The literacy rate among the Swedish newcomers eventually resulted in Chicago becoming a major center of the Swedish press, with the city serving as home to the nationally and internationally circulating *Hemlandet*, a Lutheran-oriented newspaper; and *Svenska Amerikanaren*, a secular newspaper.

The Swedes also gave back to their new home by founding many social welfare institutions including societies for widows, orphans and the unemployed; homes for the aged; and hospitals, including Augustana Hospital in 1882 and Swedish Covenant Hospital in 1886.

Though thriving Americans, these Swedish immigrants celebrated and preserved their native traditions by founding and participating in dozens of culturally based organizations, ranging from singing clubs to trade union socials as well as sending their children to Swedish language summer programs.

This Swedish American culture produced many men and women of note, including Per Samuel Peterson, the founder of Rose Hill Nursery, which by 1900 provided trees for most of the streets of Chicago at the time; and Charles R. Walgreen, the father of the massive Walgreen's chain of today, who opened the first location in Chicago in 1901.

After 1930, the Great Depression and World War II caused Swedish immigration to drop off dramatically. As a result, in the last half of the twentieth century, native Swedish speakers eventually became rare and, as longtime Swedish American families became increasingly mobile, many neighborhoods lost their distinctive Swedish flavor.

However, the local Swedish identity has not disappeared, as revealed by the 2000 census in which 123,000 Chicagoans claimed Swedish ethnicity; and as shown by the community spirit of Andersonville, a town proud of its Swedish roots. For the heritage of Chicago's Swedes is not only preserved by organizations like the Swedish American Historical Society, the Central Swedish Committee, and the Swedish American Museum, but also in the stories and traditions of each of those 123,000 Swedish American Chicagoans.

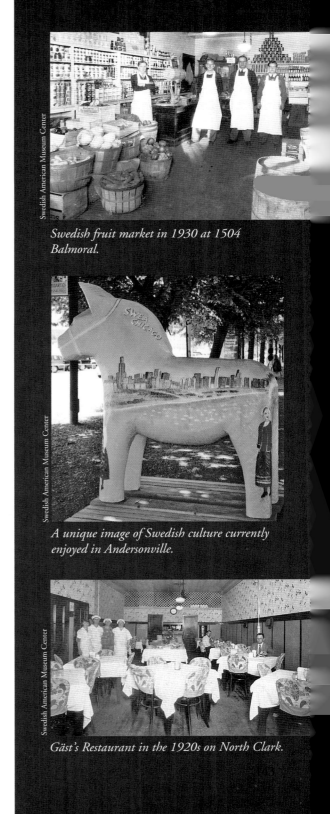

Swedish fruit market in 1930 at 1504 Balmoral.

A unique image of Swedish culture currently enjoyed in Andersonville.

Gäst's Restaurant in the 1920s on North Clark.

INGRID BERGSTROM

Born Ingrid Elisabeth Westerholm in Dala-Husby, Dalarna, Sweden in 1921, I was raised on the Dalalven River where we cultivated a vegetable garden filled with flowers and raspberries that grew large and sweet on long summer days. In 1941, I married Gosta Bergstrom on "Annandagjul" (the day after Christmas). Feeling adventurous, we set sail for America in 1947.

I remember wanting to be an actress or a Sunday School teacher. However, in New York the closest I got to acting was serving brown beans and salt pork to Greta Garbo, ice cream to Doris Day or joking with John Wayne waiting tables at the Conrad Hilton Hotel.

For job opportunity, we moved to Chicago in 1960. During the 1960s, we owned and operated the Verdandi Club Restaurant. In the '70s, we bought the Sweden Shop on Foster Avenue, across from North Park University. One day, Hazel Bergstrom, Head of Employment from the White House, walked in and invited us to Washington, D.C. Over a three-day period, we ate cherry pie with Liz Carpenter ("Ladybird" Johnson's personal secretary), visited with Vice-president Hubert Humphrey and attended a concert with the Secretary of Defense, Robert McNamara.

Encouraged by Queen Silvia of Sweden, in 2003 I published a book about my life entitled Ingrid. *God has given me a full life and I am humbled by all His blessings.*

VEAL IN DILL SAUCE

INGREDIENTS

2 lbs. breast of veal

2 tsp. salt

4 cups water

10 white peppercorns

2 cloves

1 bay leaf

2 sliced carrots

1 onion

½ cup dill, finely chopped

DILL SAUCE

2 tbsp. margarine or butter

3 tbsp. flour

1½ cups liquid from cooking the veal

½ cup light cream

1 egg yolk

Salt and white pepper

Dill, finely chopped

Fresh lemon juice or vinegar with a
bit of sugar

Place meat in a saucepan; add salt and water to cover. Bring to a boil. Remove surface scum and add the spices; cover and simmer for one hour. Add carrot, onion and dill sprigs then let simmer for another 20 minutes. Remove meat; cut into serving pieces and keep hot. Strain cooking liquid.

In a small saucepan, melt margarine (or butter). Blend in flour. Add cooking liquid and bring to a boil. Beat sauce until smooth and cook for a few minutes. Remove from heat and beat in the cream mixed with egg yolk. Season sauce with salt, pepper, dill and lemon juice. Pour it over the meat or serve sauce separately. Serve with boiled potatoes or rice.

SERVES 4

DON OLSON

We are about as "Swedish" as can be. My family originated from Smaland in south central Sweden and my wife Kay's family is from Dalarna and Värmland in the middle of Sweden.

Kay's family, the Hogfeldts, settled in Chicago in the late 1800s and her grandfather helped develop the North Park area and published the Swedish newspaper, the Missions Vannen. Her family was also instrumental in bringing North Park University (NPU) to this area in the 1890s.

Kay's folks taught me how to make Swedish potato sausage after they were too old to do so. My wife's "mormor" (mother's mother) has used this recipe for the Christmas season since the 1900s. Usually a day without potatoes is not a day. Served boiled with dill at the noonday meal, often sausage was the main dish in order to stretch the other meat used. Now that people are more affluent, more meat is used.

My folks had no desire to return to Sweden. But after my daughter visited there in 1990 through the student exchange program at NPU, we decided we had to go. We have been back six times and taught there for two semesters. We also have become involved with the Center for Scandinavian Studies at NPU and the Swedish American Historical Society.

POTATIS KORV
(POTATO SAUSAGE)

Swedish heritage means a lot not only to us but also to Chicago. It is so easy to be Swedish in this city. I love visiting the Swedish American Museum, Andersonville and partaking of Swedish customs at our church. We host choirs, bands and other performers from the "old country." Unfortunately, perhaps not so unfortunately, the clerks at the Swedish Bakery and Wikstroms are beginning to know me on a first-name basis!

INGREDIENTS

2 lbs. ground beef

2 lbs. ground pork

2 lbs. ground veal

2 large onions, finely chopped

10 large potatoes, shredded in food processor

½ lb. hog casings from meat market

1 10-oz. can beef broth

2 tbsp. salt

½ tsp. pepper

¼ tsp. allspice

. . . .

Mix all ingredients well with hands. Fry a patty or two for tasting before stuffing the casings. Adjust spices (allspice and pepper) to personal taste.

Freeze or cook by simmering for approximatly an hour.

SERVES 12-15

INGVAR WIKSTRÖM FAMILY

I grew up on a farm in Ingelstorp Sweden. It was here I learned the ethics of hard work. I learned how to cook from my mother and how to prepare foods from scratch, from their natural state. Our rice pudding (featured at right) is a traditional favorite served at Christmas time. The dish our family loves to make with leftover rice on Christmas Day is called "ris a la malta."

In 1959, as many Swedes had done before us, my wife, Alfhlild, and I moved to the United States to pursue the American dream. We had met several Swedes in Chicago on previous trips, so it was here we decided to make a new life for ourselves.

Initially, I set out working for a Swedish businessman named Andy Carlson who owned a small deli on Touhy and Clark. In 1960, we purchased this deli from Mr. Carlson and, hence, the first Wikström's Swedish Deli was born.

Wikström's Swedish Deli, in 1975, moved to Andersonville and it is here we have been greeting our customers for the past 32 years.

We are famous for our meatballs, herring, rice pudding, Glogg spices and much more.

Wikström's is now an institution in the Scandinavian community and the tradition will continue for the next generation with a new Wikström's being opened in 2008 by our daughter, Marie.

RICE PUDDING

INGREDIENTS

½ quart white rice (2 cups)

1 gallon milk

7 eggs

¼ oz. salt

1 cinnamon stick (or more to taste)

1½ pints of half & half

¾ lb. sugar

1 tbsp. vanilla extract (or Swedish vanilla sugar)

Cook rice in ½ gallon of milk with cinnamon stick(s). Heat the rest of the milk with one cup water in another pan. When rice is half done, mix in remaining milk (you now have rice porridge).

In a small bowl, combine eggs, salt, half & half, sugar and vanilla. Whip with a hand whip until well mixed then combine with the rice porridge mixture. Pour into lightly buttered pans. Rest rice pudding pan in a baking pan, then fill halfway with water to create a waterbath. Bake in pre-heated 250-degree oven for about two hours while still in waterbath. Serve cold with lingonberries.

SERVES 10-12

The parish-clerk's house in Ingelstorp, Sweden where Ingvar was born.

RESOURCES

Note: To save space, we have abbreviated the resourse *The Electronic Encyclopedia of Chicago: Chicago Historical Society* (2005), http://www.encyclopedia.chicagohistory.org to EEC plus the page number used.

Aleksas, Ambrose. *The History of Chicago Lithuanians* (Chicagos Lietuvi Istorija). Compiled by Vilius Zalpys. LGGS, 1999-2007.

Arredondo, Gabriela F., and Derek Vaillant. "Mexicans." EEC, page 824.

Cahill, Thomas. *How the Irish Saved Civilization: The Untold Story of Ireland's Heroic Role from the Fall of Rome to the Rise of Medieval Europe.* New York: Doubleday, 1995.

Cainkar, Louise. "Palestinians." EEC page 946.

Cutler, Irving. "Jews." EEC page 671.

Delgado, Louis. "Native Americans." EEC, page 874.

Diner, Hasia. *Erin's Daughters in America: Irish Immigrant Women in the Nineteenth Century.* Baltimore: Johns Hopkins University Press, 1983.

"Ethnic History of Bridgeport." A historic preservation project of architecture, art history, and urban planning students at The University of Illinois at Chicago. Done in cooperation with the Commission on Chicago Landmarks, Department of Planning and Development. http://www.uic.edu/orgs/LockZero/

Funchion, Michael F. "Irish Chicago: Church, Homeland, Politics, and Class – The Shaping of an Ethnic Group, 1870-1900." In Ethnic Chicago, edited by Melvin G. Holli and Peter d'A. Jones. Grand Rapids, MI: William B. Eerdmans Publishing Company, 1984.

Ganakos, Alexa. *Greektown Chicago: Its History – Its Recipes.* St. Louis: G. Bradley Publishing, Inc., 2005.

Geographia Asia. "A Concise History of India." http://www.geographia.com/india/india02.html.

González, Mirza L., "Cubans." EEC, page 356.

Gualtieri, Sarah. "Lebanese." EEC, page 732.

Gualtieri, Sarah. "Syrians." EEC, page 1226.

Gustafson, Anita Olson. "Swedes." EEC, page 1222.

Hanania, Ray. *Arabs of Chicagoland.* Charleston, SC: Arcadia Publishing, 2005.

Harzig, Christiane. "Germans." EEC, page 512.

Johnson, Brandon. "Eastern Rite Catholics." EEC, page 2189.

Keil, Harmut. *German Workers in Chicago: A Documentary History of Working-Class Culture from 1850 to World War I* (Working Class in American History). Urbana, IL: University of Illinois Press, 1988.

Kerr, Louise Ano Nuevo. "Mexican Chicago: Chicano Assimilation Aborted, 1939-1954." *In Ethnic Chicago*, edited by Melvin G. Holli and Peter d'A. Jones. Grand Rapids, MI: William B. Eerdmans Publishing Company, 1984.

Kopan, Andrew. T. "Greek Survival in Chicago: The Role of Ethnic Education, 1890-1980." In *Ethnic Chicago*, edited by Melvin G. Holli and Peter d'A. Jones. Grand Rapids, MI: William B. Eerdmans Publishing Company, 1984.

Kopan, Andrew T. "Greeks." EEC, page 548.

Lai, Vinay. "Indians." EEC, page 635.

Manning, Christopher. "African Americans." EEC, page 27.

Mehrotra, Ajay K. "Pakistanis." EEC, page 944.

Nebraska Department of Education. "Laws that Isolated and Impoverished the Irish." http://www.nde.state.ne.us/SS/irish/unit_1.html.

Pacyga, Dominic A. "Poles." EEC, page, 982.

Pérez, Gina M. "Puerto Ricans." EEC, page 1027.

Senn, Alfred Erich. "Lithuanians." EEC, page 757.

Skerrett, Ellen. "Irish." EEC, page 652.

Skilnik, Robert. *Beer: A History of Brewing in Chicago.* Fort Lee, NJ: Barricade Books, 2006.

Steffes, Tracy. "Chinese." EEC, page 285.

University of Minnesota Law School. "Laws in Ireland for the Suppression of Popery commonly known as the Penal Laws." University of Minnesota.http://www.law.umn.edu/irishlaw/.

Vecoli, Rudolph J. "Italians." EEC, page 658.

Zurawski, Joseph W. *Polish Chicago: Our History – Our Recipes.* St. Louis: G. Bradley Publishing, Inc., 2007.

Acknowledgements

The writers and production staff of *The Foods of Chicago: A Delicious History* would like to express our sincere gratitude to all the wonderful individuals who contributed recipes to this book. You not only donated your delicious recipes, but you also opened your homes and places of business to us. You shared personal stories and generously gave of your time, making this project a true team effort. We at G. Bradley Publishing are privileged to have been able to work with you.

We would also like to thank the staff of WTTW11 and the producers of the documentary *The Foods of Chicago: A Delicious History* for bringing this exciting project to us and for giving us your excellent insights and guidance. In particular, we acknowledge Geoffrey Baer, Dan Protess, Jerry Liwanag, Susan Godfrey, Kathleen Singleton and Pavan Bapu.

With regard to the historical sections of the book, the writer would like to express her appreciation and thanks to all the historical contributors on this project. Thank you for your editorial suggestions, knowledge and your historical and cultural insights. This project would not have been possible without you.

In particular, we express our thanks to the following individuals in alphabetical order:

Karin Abercrombie, Executive Director, Swedish American Museum Center

Maureen Abood

Karin Andersson, Curator, Swedish American Museum Center

Julie Bartlett

Laura Frankel

Alexa Ganakos

Cesar Garza

Peggy Glowacki, University of Illinois-Chicago

Ray Hanania

Wilbert Jones, President, Healthy Concepts, Inc.

Bruce Kraig, Ph.D., President, Culinary Historians of Chicago

Gene Moy, M.A., President of the Chicago Chinese American Historical Society

Donald Olson

Tina Padilla

Kantha Shelke, Ph.D., Principal, Corvus Blue, LLC, Chicago.

Robert Skilnik

Dorene Wiese, President and Professor of NAES College

Marie Wikström

Carmen Yee

Joseph W. Zurawski, M.A.

For the recipe section of the book, we extend our warmest thanks to Catherine Lambrecht of the Chicago Foodways Roundtable who reviewed and edited each recipe in this book. To Catherine; it was an absolute pleasure working with you. The production schedule of this book was brutal, and you came through without batting an eyelash. We cannot thank you enough!

Last, but definitely not least, we would like to thank our brilliant photographers. It is you who has made this book so appealing!

To Katherine Bish, our food and personality photographer, your work here was essential in making the book the success it is. We gave you a challenging schedule of almost 40 photo shoots in a short time, and you gave us Chicago in living, breathing, exquisite color.

We would also like to thank our gifted Chicagoland photographers. We came knocking on your doors with little time and an almost nonexistent budget, and you gave us magic. Thank you for your generosity and talent. We wish you all the best and are looking forward to seeing your work again very soon. We would specifically like to thank, in alphabetical order:

Jeremy Atherton

Samuel Barnett

Sean Benham

Sean Birmingham

Luis Cabrera

Dominic Candeloro

Sam Daou

Chris Diers

Richie Diesterheft

Stephen Gay

Phineas Jones

Tina Mete

Dimitri William Moore

Jay Morthland

Barb Murphy

Bill Richert

Marshall Rosenthal

Stanley Wlodkowski

Wojciech Wierzewski

Finally, we thank the recipe contributors for their photo contributions. Your generosity has made this book personal and has given it heart and soul.

We also wish to express our gratitude to the

following individuals and organizations for their outstanding photograph submissions. Through your efforts, we can see history chronicled in this book. In alphabetical order, we recognize the following:

Arab American View Newspaper
Balzekas Museum of Lithuanian Culture
Cliff Carlson / Irish American News
Dominic Candeloro
Chicago History Museum
Ray Hanania
Hanania Enterprises, Ltd.
Valerie Harris

Irish American Heritage Center
Italian Cultural Center at Casa Italia
Jesse White Tumbling Team
Carlos Peynetsa
Polish Museum of America
Peig Reid
South Asian Friendship Center
Swedish American Museum Center
University of Illinois-Chicago
Dorene Wiese
Jesse White, Illinois Secretary of State
WTTW11

Tradition is passed on to our youth.

Bill Richert

EPILOGUE

The face of Chicago is constantly changing. This comes, in part, from the ongoing stream of immigrants arriving in this dynamic city. We continue to thrive in the opportunities this nation and great city provides. We have much to share and celebrate. As we look back with justifiable pride on our past, the greater is our desire to assure a bright and rewarding future for our children.

Chicago is vast and rich in cultural diversity. Divided geographically by the south side, west side and north side, Chicago citizens are as proud to be Chicagoans as they are to identify with their neighborhood or community of origin.

In their respective communities, immigrants to the Windy City have risen to positions of prominence in business and leadership roles. United in spirit, they have established churches, organizations, museums and schools to keep alive their individual cultural heritage.

Worldwide, food is the common denominator. To love another by offering what you have, usually food, is understood by all. Sitting down to a shared meal is something which unites us rather than divides us. We are defined by our past. Historians remind us that food says a lot about who we are and who others think we are. When citizens and visitors to Chicago experience new and different cultures, they often first think of the foods which define a certain community and its population. Just as essential as a visit to the Sears Tower or Wrigley Field is a memorable dining experience, especially in an ethnic restaurant or neighborhood. One of the benefits of Chicago is that you can symbolically travel to dozens of different countries without leaving the city's borders. Thus the "melting pot" of America is served well on the streets of Chicago.

It is hoped that this keepsake book of photos, history and food will be a remembrance of our collective accomplishments and gives us the momentum to continue to preserve our rich past for future generations.